Tim Merriman and Lisa Brochu

*The History of*
HERITAGE INTERPRETATION
*in the United States*

THE
NATIONAL
ASSOCIATION FOR
INTERPRETATION

P.O. Box 2246
Fort Collins, CO 80522

NAI is a private nonprofit [501(c)3] organization and
professional association. NAI's mission is: "Inspiring
leadership and excellence to advance heritage
interpretation as a profession." For information, visit
www.interpnet.com.

ISBN 1–879931–19–2

# CONTENTS

# FOREWORD

When I was small, I would impatiently sit with relatives at the dining table as they recounted stories from years gone by. The stories had nothing to do with the swing set I could see out the window, or my cousins with whom I was eager to play. I usually slid off my chair quietly to escape the story-telling that seemed to have little to do with me.

As I got older, I began to relish the tales my grandparents, aunts, uncles, and parents shared around a bowl of pasta or a plate full of creamy cannolis. The stories began to connect me with my past, and gave me pride in my heritage.

It wasn't until I had worked as an interpreter for several years when I began to be curious about the evolution of interpretation as a profession. Since I'd come from the ranks of biology and natural resource study, I had little formal training in interpretation and knew nothing about its history.

At first I searched for the company of historic women guides and naturalists. Working in a male-dominated field at the time, I was curious to know if other women felt the same calling to share their love for birds, wildflowers, woodlands, and marshes. My readings took me to Gene Stratton-Porter, Cordelia Stanwood, Alice Eastwood, and Althea Sherman. From there I dug into Enos Mills, John Muir, and Freeman Tilden. Their stories began to connect me with my chosen profession and its roots.

With every story I read, the power of interpretation and its ability to connect people to the earth's natural and cultural heritage became ever clearer. Each book was like a window opening, and I was eager to discover more.

It is fitting that the National Association for Interpretation has assembled this volume. It is a look back at the various aspects of interpretation, the professional organizations it has fostered, and the trends and challenges it faces.

Let it be your window to the past and future of the proud profession of interpretation—and may it encourage you to seek out your own research and dialogue.

"The past, the present, and the future are really one: they are today."
—Harriet Beecher Stowe

Evie Kirkwood
President, National Association for Interpretation
Director, St. Joseph County Parks, Indiana

# PREFACE

Bill Randall, a vice-president of the Association of Interpretive Naturalists in the 1980s, was a professor of interpretation and department chair at the University of Massachusetts and a champion of recording the history of the profession. He hoped to write a book sharing his personal knowledge about Freeman Tilden and other interpretive pioneers after he retired, but sadly did not have enough years left in his life to complete the work. Losing Bill and others in our field in recent years reminds us of the value of recording some of the milestones in the growth of our profession, and so we offer this book to carry on his spirit of enthusiasm for remembering our roots.

As you read, you may think, "they missed telling the story about . . ." or "I wonder why that great photo of a critical meeting wasn't included in this book." As we researched written records and the memories of colleagues and wrote about what we knew, we also became acutely aware of the gaps in our knowledge. Very often, history happens right under our noses, but we neglect to take a key photo, save an important document, or record significant details as they occur. Consequently, we deliberately kept the first edition of this book at a low print number. We hope to go to print with a second edition in just a couple of years that we hope will include that great photo you will send us or an important story that fills in one of our gaps. If you can send us that fitting addition to the story of how heritage interpretation has evolved and changed over the years, we will be happy to include it in the second edition and recognize your contribution.

We would like to thank the authors who participated in this edition as essayists. Their diverse views about the shaping of the profession enriched our understanding of the subject. We hope the varied essays will have a similar value for you.

The tradition of interpretation—helping people connect with nature and history—seems as old as humankind, but people are discovering interpretation as a profession each and every day. They become interpreters as docents and volunteers at zoos, museums, nature centers, and aquariums. They are hired out of college into seasonal positions with parks or tourism organizations. Biologists and historians start with the research side of the field and move toward the communication side of it. We hope they all discover, as we have, that many of the thoughts of Enos Mills, May Thielgaard Watts, or any of the other pioneers of interpretation are as relevant and useful today as they were for interpreters 50 or 100 years ago.

We each carry with us the traditions and understandings of the past and add what we learn each year that is new and important. The history of the profession is not only about what has happened, but is more a study of change as the profession continues to grow and evolve. As an interpreter, you can add to the history of the profession by becoming an active participant in its future. We welcome your thoughts and insights along the way.

# 1
## KEEPERS OF THE CULTURE

Many professions have historical roots in the most common of aboriginal community roles. The tribal leader in a modern context may be an attorney, judge, or politician. The herbalist or witch doctor roles of tribal life evolved into modern medical professionals of hundreds of kinds. Heritage interpreters also have roots in tribal life. As keepers of culture, they protect the natural environment and social structure of their surroundings by encouraging ongoing stewardship of those resources. Protection of natural and cultural resources is everybody's responsibility, but interpreters help people better understand their connections to the world around them. Civilization is based on continuous improvement of the human condition within the context of the known world. Leaders, parents, and teachers share life's lessons with each successive generation. Before written texts collected societal memories, oral tradition preserved cultural history. Interpreters are not doing something new. They have refined age-old traditions with the development of definitions, standards of practice, and ethics.

Long before interpretation existed in a professional framework, the oldest and wisest members of the tribe were the keepers of the culture, the experts. Experience molded good teachers. During China's dynastic periods, a person who had lived eight decades could advise even the emperor.[1] The wisdom gained from living a long life had value. Cultural anthropologists suggest that tribal or village members developed special skills as communities evolved and required more complex leadership. Many cultures described the roles of shamans, bards, jesters, and storytellers as entertainers who carried oral history from village to village and decade to decade. Folk songs that evolved over time can often be traced for hundreds of years. These songs recorded significant events worthy of being remembered. They documented the tragedies, frustrations, and pain of arduous lives in mines, factories, and farms. They were stories of love, joy, sorrow, and daily dramas set to music, and often had a message or a moral. Songs and stories captured the most complex thoughts and beliefs made easy to remember. The hunter's tale of prowess on the plains, the jester's jokes about the court, and the herbalist's cure for the "scours" may have foreshadowed our profession.

In 2000 Keith Dewar wrote an article entitled "An Incomplete History of Interpretation from the Big Bang"[2] for the *International Journal of Heritage Studies*. He quotes Herodotus in 460 B.C. referring to his "interpreter," translated from ancient Greek as "he who explains." He also mentions freelance guides at the pyramids of Egypt and the prevalence of priest/interpreters in literature for two millennia. He wrote:

**Herodotus**

> . . . the ancient guide shared with modern descendants the inability to stop, once he was launched on his patter . . . .. It was not only that guides never stopped talking; it was also what they talked about . . . .. Even worse, whatever facts they did offer they like to embroider with fancy, knowing that the average hearer had no way of checking up.

In 1780 Bryan Merryman, a bachelor Irish math teacher in his 30s, wrote *The Midnight Court* in Gaelic.[3] It was an epic poem decrying the plight of unmarried maidens who deserved the chance to have a family and rear children. At the time it was considered bawdy and brazen, discussing the sexual habits of priests and maidens. It was widely memorized by bards and repeated over the past two centuries, resurfacing as a play in recent times. Works of art have always played a role in social evolution as storytellers carried cultural questions and controversies from village to village.

It is easy, while telling stories at a park campfire, to imagine that the interpreter would have done this same thing if born many centuries earlier. Some people seem drawn to the oral tradition for reasons that may be hard to explain. The urge to share a love of history and stories of nature with others could be a holdover from times past when survival relied on knowledge, hope and faith gleaned from the collective wisdom of the group. Though professional interpreters share their stories for pay, most choose the profession for other reasons. Few interpretive jobs pay so well that people would take the job for just that reason.

Costumed interpretation and living history employ drama to relate stories in modern interpretive settings. The art of the actor has been valued for several millennia in human culture, since Thespis of Athens used both dialogue and a chorus or dance to convey myths, legends, and lore of the times in Greek tragedy as far back as 535 BC.[4] These performances attracted audiences of 10,000 or more. The ancient Greeks honored both the traditional stories and fictional dramas of contemporary writers.

Voyageurs and mountain men served as hunters, guides, scouts, and translators. They helped many pioneers, explorers, mapmakers, and artists find their way westward across the North American continent. These unique individuals became natural and cultural history guides of the most serious kind. Their skills kept people alive and changed the course of history forever. The modern roles of interpreters may lack that immediacy, but interpreters sometimes save lives and protect others from injury when their abilities help people avoid mistakes, get oriented, and stay away from risky behavior. Guiding is as simple as leading people down a trail and as complex as helping them have a life-changing experience. Perhaps it has always been so.

*A candle loses nothing by lighting another candle.*

—Erin Majors[5]

# 2

# EXPLORERS OF THE EARTH

*I'll interpret the rocks, learn the language of flood, storm, and the avalanche. I'll acquaint myself with the glaciers and wild gardens, and get as near the heart of the world as I can.*

—John Muir[6]

## Trailblazers

No matter their century or country of origin, explorers have one thing in common. They want to know more about the Earth, its lands, and its inhabitants. They study and record their thoughts and memories in a variety of ways. Norsemen, voyageurs, and frontiersmen who visited North America in past centuries seemed driven as much by curiosity as need. Charles Darwin traveled the coast of South America on the *HMS Beagle* at age 22, one of the few long trips of his life and one of the most important. Darwin intended to become a clergyman or physician in the footsteps of his ancestors, but instead became a naturalist with a mapmaking exploration of the New World. Darwin took ideas sown by his physician grandfather, Erasmus Darwin, as inspiration for his famous book, *Origin of the Species.*[7] Darwin's ideas stimulated discussion and arguments that continue even today about how life changes on this planet. He took examples from nature and illuminated larger principles from them. Was he an interpreter? Darwin wrote in his autobiography that "the voyage of the *Beagle* . . .

**Charles Darwin**

has been by far the most important event of my life and has determined my whole career."[8] He never left England after returning from his five-year journey, but he lectured and wrote about what he learned on the trip for the rest of his life.

In the United States and Canada a variety of explorers, mapmakers, biologists, and artists interpreted the shrinking frontier to those in cities and communities. Often they left the comforts of the city or civilization behind to explore new territory and record what they saw. These individuals were certainly not interpreters in the sense that the profession is pursued today, but like the herbalists who preceded physicians and pharmacists, they were people with similar interests to those working today in the natural and cultural history fields. Their explorations were not done with comfort, safety, security, and foreknowledge about their experiences, but they did interpret what they saw and the profession is richer for their efforts. A few specific individuals warrant mention because their activities led to similar roles now performed in the interpretive field.

Artists like George Catlin, Frederic Remington, and Charles Russell were the interpreters of the American frontier. They transformed images from their experiences with tribal cultures and cowboys on the trail into art, providing a personal interpretation of life in the American West for less adventurous people who had yet to venture from their homes in the east. The works of these artists still endure as unique studies of their time, before cameras became common. Catlin's *Letters and Notes on the Manners, Customs, and Condition of the North American Indians* have been described as "one of the finest studies that have ever been written."[9] He has been regarded by some as a proto-anthropologist, a naturalist and historian whose words and paintings interpret the West of the early to mid-1800s with empathy and accuracy. Once when Catlin

**George Catlin paints a chief at the base of the Rocky Mountains.**

was critical of Sioux practices of torturing prisoners, he reported that a Sioux chief commented on the white practice of hanging criminals as "choked . . . to death like dogs." The Sioux chief commented that, "he had seen them (white settlers) whip their little children—a thing that is very cruel . . .." His notes give us an understanding of the sophistication of Native American leaders often lacking in the more popular press that frequently generalized a description of all Indians as savages.

In the late 1800s and early 1900s Charles "Charlie" Marion Russell captured his views and interpretations of Native Americans and cowboys of Montana in more than 4,000 works of art.[10] His paintings and bronzes provoke our desire to understand more about that time. These enduring visual images tell powerful stories of adventure, challenge, and intrigue.

TIM GIBSON, USACE

**US Army Corps of Engineers living history interpreters recreate moments from the Lewis and Clark expedition.**

Frederic Remington of Canton, New York, lived from 1861 to 1909 when complications from appendicitis took his life at 48 years of age. His drawings and illustrations for magazines including *Harper's Weekly, Harper's Monthly, Boy's Life, Outing, Century, Cosmopolitan,* and *Collier's* created indelible images of the American West along with many stories of high adventure. As a sculptor, his 22 bronzes endure as visions of the life of cowboys and Native Americans on the plains. He said of his motivations to explore as he wrote and drew:

> I knew the wild riders and the vacant land were about to vanish forever, and the more I considered the subject, the bigger the forever loomed…. I began to try to record some facts around me, and the more I looked, the more the panorama unfolded.[11]

Interpreters today value journaling as a way to preserve observations when having a new experience with nature or history. The written records of William Clark, Merriwether Lewis and several other members of the Voyage of Discovery from 1804 to 1806 left impressions of what the journey was like, as they traversed the western U.S. in search of an overland trail to the Pacific Ocean. The messages were not written for a reader, but more as reminders to the explorers of what was occurring each day of the journey. Two hundred years later their journal notes help interpret the bicentennial celebration of their trek through vivid verbal pictures of the people and places they encountered, spiced with the cultural perspectives of those days.

### Naturalists and Nature Guides

Born the son of a Scottish clergyman in 1838, John Muir[12] moved to Wisconsin as a boy and endured a challenging relationship with his fundamentalist father. He went to work as a young man in Indiana in a machine shop and proved himself an able inventor. An accident blinded him in one eye and for weeks his other eye was sympathetically blind, leaving him to adjust to a potential life without vision.

When his sight eventually returned, he left the machine shop forever and trekked from Louisville, Kentucky to Savannah, Georgia in 1868. As he continued his wanderings, he found a spiritual and physical home for six summers in California in what would, largely through his good efforts, become Yosemite National Park. Muir served as a guide for Ralph Waldo Emerson who urged him to leave the wilderness to share with others what he had learned. After camping with Robert Underwood Johnson, editor of *Century* magazine, in Tuolomne Valley in 1989, Muir wrote a series of articles that proved invaluable in helping to move Yosemite Valley from state to federal ownership and management.

**President Theodore Roosevelt and John Muir, pictured here in Yosemite in 1903, were friends.**

Muir's passion for wilderness and protection of beautiful places continued to grow in Martinez, California, where he lived as an orchard owner. He was a friend of President Theodore Roosevelt and became a man of great influence in his time. Muir cofounded the Sierra Club to underscore his belief that nature appreciation required an understanding of the bigger ideas within it. He was acknowledged by many influential people of his day as one who guided and inspired an early movement to preserve wilderness for the future. When mountaineer Rheinhold Wessner was asked why the Alps were so developed with cities and railroads while mountains of the American West were not, he said, "You had Muir."

John Muir became an important spokesman for heritage resources in North America, but elsewhere, others had influence in their own lands. In Japan, a peasant farmer angered by pollution in the Watarase River challenged the emperor of the time to help protect people from the dangers posed by copper mining. Despite being jailed for his impertinence, Tanaka Shozo (1841–1913)[13] continued to inspire local farmers to resist attempts to impound polluted waters. Shortly after his death at age 72, the farmers' movement succumbed to governmental desires to build a dam that would claim their village and farms, but Shozo is remembered as an early conservationist of great importance. He is often quoted as saying, "The care of rivers is not a question of rivers, but of the human heart."

Tanaka Shozo was an important force in his time for environmental protection in Japan. A university now bears his name in recognition of his contributions as a pioneer of conservation. His written words endure in the book *Ox Against the Storm*, reminding interpreters that making emotional connections is vital in encouraging people to be stewards of heritage resources. It takes more than facts to engage people in lasting ways.

The person often described as "Father of Heritage Interpretation" grew up in Fort Scott, Kansas, just after the Civil War was over.[14] At age 14 Enos Mills set out for Estes Park, Colorado, to improve his health. He alternated work for family friends on a guest ranch near Estes Park with seasonal work in the mines of Butte, Montana. Over a period of three years he built a log cabin on a mountainside near Estes Park with a magnificent view of Long's Peak, the tallest mountain in the area.

During a visit to California, Mills became acquainted with John Muir after they met serendipitously on the beach. Much as Emerson had encouraged Muir, Muir took young Mills to Yosemite Valley and suggested that he become an articulate advocate for protecting wild places by writing and speaking. Mills took that advice seriously and became one of several people instrumental in the creation of Rocky Mountain National Park.

Mills wrote 20 books in his 52 years of life and many of them are still considered to be authoritative resources. His book on grizzly bears was based upon hundreds of hours of tracking bears on foot. *The Story of a Thousand Year Old Pine*[15] is an interpretive story of his dissection of a giant ponderosa pine near Mesa Verde National Park. The tree, cut by lumberjacks for timber, was left behind because it was hollow. Saddened by the turn of events, Mills sought to reveal its story as a way to make meaningful use of its death. He described each scar and charred area evident in the rings of the tree, unveiling its history of 1,000 years. This story remains an excellent example for interpretive students of the meanings that can be found within any single thing.

At a relatively young age, Mills founded a nature guiding school. He also operated his own lodge and guide service in the Estes Park area until his death in 1920. He led groups up Longs Peak more than 250 times and knew the trail intimately, often taking

PAUL CAPUTO

**With Longs Peak looming in the background, Enda Mills Kiley, pictured here at 86 years old in 2004, holds her favorite photo of the man who fought to help found Rocky Mountain National Park, her father Enos Mills.**

special groups in moonlight. His book, *Adventures of a Nature Guide*[16] has endured as an inspirational view of this emerging profession from a practitioner of great skill and experience. Mills foresaw the need for the profession and predicted it would grow and prosper when he said, ". . . may the tribe increase."

Enda Mills Kiley was the only child of Enos and Esther Burnell Mills, one of the first female guides. True to her genes, Enda continued the work of her parents in her middle and senior years in the Estes Park area. Though only three years of age at his death, she kept his legacy alive. Many of the concepts taught today in interpretive training have their roots in the field-tested ideas of Enos Mills. Mills said, "A guide's chief aim is to arouse a permanent interest in nature's ways, and this by illuminating big principles."

At a time in the early 20th century when women were not often allowed access to professions despite their abilities, Mills encouraged women as nature guides and devoted a chapter of "Adventures" to extolling their skills. Mills more than any other individual left a written legacy of his beliefs that reflect many of the most important values of our profession.

These pioneers of interpretation did not necessarily think of their profession as heritage interpretation but their work reflected the passions that still fire interpreters today. Many others also helped pave the way for the profession. Their contributions are no less important, but may not be as readily recognized from surviving literature and histories of their times.

# 3

## THE GROWING PROFESSION

Early interpreters may not have seen themselves as building a profession. They were in pursuit of their work as artists, surveyors, historians or naturalists. Enos Mills, more than anyone, had the vision for a profession of guides who would help reveal the richness of heritage resources to those who came to the nation's treasured places. He believed that his role as a guide and a trainer of other guides would grow and expand well beyond himself one day.

Almost simultaneously in the late 1800s, multiple federal agencies developed in the United States with the charge of protecting and conserving natural and cultural resources for the public good. The National Park Service led the way in the use of interpretation to help the public understand and appreciate those resources.

**Enos Mills**

### National Park Service and USDA Forest Service

U.S. Army soldiers guarded the newly created Yellowstone National Park in 1886. Occasionally, they interpreted the site to visitors by giving "cone talks." Robert Shankland[17] described early efforts at interpretation:

> In the early days at Yellowstone, the tourist who neglected to stuff himself in advance at the encyclopedias was liable to have a dark time

of it among the volcanic phenomena. There was little on-the-spot enlightenment. Most stagecoach drivers liked to descant to the customers, but in a vein of bold invention. A few voluble guides worked out of the hotels; they cruelly punished the natural sciences. Under the regulations the guides could charge no fees. They did well, however, on tips, which they induced by a classic method: every audience harbored an unacknowledged accomplice, who at the end of a guide's remarks voiced resounding appreciation and, with a strong look around, extended a generous cash award.

Guiding services proved popular throughout the park system, but guides were not always available.

In 1905 Frank Pinkley, custodian of the Casa Grande Ruin Reservation (later Casa Grande National Monument) in Arizona Territory, pioneered another category of interpretation when he assembled a sampling of prehistoric artifacts recovered from archeological excavation in the ruin. Pinkley's display has been called the forerunner of national park museum exhibits. The year before, 1st Lt. Henry F. Pipes, a surgeon with the 9th Cavalry stationed in Yosemite National Park, laid out paths and labeled 36 species of plants near Wawona as part of an arboretum. This natural exhibit was abandoned after it was discovered to lie on private land, and the military superintendent's plan for an adjoining museum and library building was not realized. By 1915 Yosemite did have what it called a museum, in the form of a flora and fauna specimen collection exhibited in the headquarters building.

Of the several forms of early park explanatory media, publications reached the largest audience. In 1911 Laurence F. Schmeckebier, the Department of the Interior's clerk in charge of publications, asked the superintendents of the larger parks to submit material for a series of handbooks containing basic information on access, accommodations, and the like. A second handbook series promoted by Schmeckebier and written by Smithsonian Institution and U.S. Geological Survey scientists interpreted major park features. Booklets included *The Secret of the Big Trees: Yosemite Sequoia and General Grant National Parks* (1913) by Ellsworth Huntington, *Origin of Scenic Features of Glacier National Park* (1914) by N. R. Campbell, *Mount Rainier and Its Glaciers* (1914) by F. E. Matthes, and *Fossil Forests of Yellowstone National Park* (1914) by F. H. Knowlton. In a 1912 article in *Popular Science Monthly*, "The National Parks from the Educational and Scientific Side," Schmeckebier publicized the values forthcoming from popular study and professional research.

Barry Mackintosh, NPS historian, describes other early efforts to interpret NPS sites and resources in great detail.[18] This fascinating history gives a thorough accounting of the groundwork NPS employees provided in the interpretive field.

NPS Director Stephen Mather installed naturalists in Lake Tahoe resorts in 1918 and in Yosemite in 1919. Dr. Harold Bryant and Dr. Loye H. Miller served as program naturalists in Yosemite National Park, where nature talks and campfire programs proved popular during summer seasons. These groundbreaking interpreters served without pay until 1923 when Dr. Bryant was appointed as a seasonal park ranger. Dr. Bryant, a graduate of Pomona College and University of California at Berkeley in zoology with an ornithology specialization, worked for California Fish and Game Commission as a lecturer and field trip leader. In 1925 he became the first director of the Yosemite School of Field Natural History, where naturalists trained with an emphasis on field experiences instead of books. Bryant soon became assistant director of the Branch of Research and

**Stephen Mather was the first director of the National Park Service.**

Education and served under Horace Albright and Arno B. Cammerer. He finished his NPS career after 14 years as superintendent of Grand Canyon National Park and remained justifiably proud of having had an important role in development of interpretive programming for NPS.

The U.S. Department of Agriculture's Forest Service may have fielded its first interpreter in the form of a cartoon bear in a national ad campaign. Fears of catastrophic forest fires during World War II prompted the Forest Service to use Uncle Sam as a spokesman for protecting forests from fire. Bambi was recruited next with Walt Disney's permission to use the cartoon character to discourage unsafe behavior with fires. Albert Staehle drew the first Smokey Bear poster on August 9, 1944.[19] Named after "Smokey" Joe Martin, the assistant fire chief in New York City, Smokey Bear became one of the most successful icons of conservation messages ever created. In 1950 an orphaned black bear found in the Lincoln National Forest in New Mexico during the Capitan Gap fire became the physical

Remember–Only YOU can PREVENT FOREST FIRES!

embodiment of Smokey. Smokey spent the remaining 25 years of his life at at the National Zoo in Washington, D.C.

On the ground the Forest Service fielded its first interpreter in the Tahoe National Forest in 1961[20] when Robert K. Morris began leading hikes and conducting evening programs and was appointed one of the first visitor information officers on a Forest Service district. Once again, resorts in the Tahoe area proved to be an excellent public testing ground as they had been for NPS many years before. It is no wonder that the backdrop provided by Lake Tahoe's spectacular scenery set an exceptional stage for these and other early agency interpreters, but the west was not the singular stronghold in the development of interpretive programming designed to enhance the visitor experience.

## Naturalist Programs in the Eastern U.S.

Naturalists like John James Audubon, Professor Louis Agassiz, Alexander Wilson, and William Beebe were noted for their art and published journals, but in the early 1900s many parks systems in the eastern United States featured those same naturalists as public speakers.

Ernest Seton Thompson[21] wrote and illustrated books for youngsters such as *Lobo, Rag and Vixen, Wild Animals I have Known, Lives of the Hunted* (1901), and *Animal Heroes* (1905). He was the 10th son of Scottish parents living in England. After emigrating to Canada, the family settled in the Ontario wilderness for four difficult years and then moved to Toronto. Thompson became known as a naturalist, eventually producing more than 40 books. Thompson brought the Boy Scout movement to the United States and served as chief scout for five years. His authoritative writings, beautiful illustrations, and over 300 public presentations inspired a whole new generation of young naturalists in the early 20th century.

While many individuals helped people connect with nature and history directly through guided hikes in outdoor settings, a variety of institutions began to serve as urban collections of wonders from more remote locations. Arboreta, botanical gardens, zoos, and similar organizations developed around the world. Bartram's Gardens in 1728 was one of the first, followed by Philadelphia Botanical Society (1806), Arnold Arboretum at Harvard (1876), New York Botanical Garden (1891), and the Brooklyn Botanical Garden (1910).[22]

Museums created important collections of natural and cultural history specimens and artifacts, supporting strong research and curatorial programs. The British Museum began after Parliament acquired the private collections of Sir Hans Sloane following his death in 1753. Smithsonian Institution (1846), the Museum of Natural History and Comparative Anatomy at Harvard (1859), the Peabody Museum of Natural History at Yale (1866), and the New York Museum of Natural History (1870) became important institutional collections and Boston created the first museum devoted to children in 1889. The significance of these and other collections throughout the country gave rise to the American Association of Museums in 1906. Educational programs and scientific lecture programs developed over time, though interpretation was not the word used to describe programming until recently.

Zoos opened throughout the U.S. from the late 1800s onward. Some of the earliest facilities included the Cincinnati Zoo (1875), Philadelphia Zoo (1876), New York Zoological Park (1988), National Zoological Park (1890), and the New

York Zoological Gardens (1899). Zoos, like museums, primarily identified education as a program for school children that eventually evolved into interpretive services for more diverse publics.

Zurich-born Johann Heinrich Pestalozzi had great influence in the early 1800s through his passion for nature-based education. He is quoted as saying:

> I wish to wrest education from the outworn order of doddering old teaching hacks as well as from the new-fangled order of cheap, artificial teaching tricks, and entrust it to the eternal powers of nature herself, to the light which God has kindled and kept alive in the hearts of fathers and mothers, to the interests of parents who desire their children grow up in favour with God and with men.[23]

**Johann Heinrich Pestalozzi**

His 1801 book, *How Gertrude Teaches her Children*, had great influence on teacher education in the United States at the Oswego Training School for Teachers. The New Harmony community in southwestern Indiana was also an important center for notable scientists from 1820 to 1860, including William Maclure, the father of geology; Thomas Say, the father of entomology; and Joseph Neef who brought the Pestalozzian method to the U.S. Object-based teaching spread throughout the country, peaking in the late 1880s and laying the foundation for a revival of interest in nature education in the 1900s.[24]

## Urban Park Naturalists

Around the country, museums provided housing for important collections of historic artifacts, while emerging programs allowed people to interact directly with nature. Harland H. Ballard founded The Agassiz Association[25] in 1875 in honor of Professor Louis Agassiz to encourage nature study and research among young people. Wilbur S. Jackman at Cook County Normal wrote *Nature Study for Common Schools* and edited the third yearbook of the National Society of the Study of Education on nature study. The nature study movement became prominent at Cornell University in the late 1890s. Stanford had a similar reputation as the "Cornell of the West" under the leadership of Cornell graduate David Starr Jordan, first president of the California school.

Youth organizations and camping programs also promoted nature study. Edward Howe Forbush started a nature camp in New Hampshire in 1885. William W. Price's Camp Agassiz at Fallen Leaf Lake near Lake Tahoe began in 1896 and lasted for 20 years. Seton's 1896 Woodcraft Indians program was followed by Daniel Carter Beard's Sons of Daniel Boone along with the work of Lord Baden

Powell's Boy Scouts (1907) and Lady Powell's Girl Guides in England. The Museum of Natural History trained George Gladden's Boy Scout Troop to lead visually impaired people through the museum in 1918, offering one of the first known programs for a disabled population.

Many park systems around the U.S. hired a single naturalist who then paved the way for an entire staff of naturalists. Hired primarily for their natural history knowledge and outdoor skills, these naturalists tended to be skilled communicators as well. Cleveland Metroparks hired Arthur B. Williams in 1930. Typical of the naturalists of the time, he used his camera and journal to collect stories of the parks and share them with audiences. He also built the first three nature centers in the system. Eleven years later, Cleveland Metroparks hired their first female naturalist, Alice Porter.

The Works Progress Administration (WPA) and Civilian Conservation Corps (CCC) in the 1930s were programs that increased interpretive programming in state and national parks around the U.S., but the start of World War II in 1941 reversed this trend and eliminated many of these new programs. Howard "Howdy" Weaver reported that nine states had park naturalist programs from 1949 to 1951 with the strongest programs in Indiana and California.[26]

Research about conservation education and interpretive programming grew in the 1930s and 1940s, documented by Grant Sharpe's 1982 book.[27]

> Theses, mostly doctoral, devoted to park and park-related interpretive programs were written by Ann L. Steger, John R. Arnold, Babette I. Brown, Minter Westfall, George W. Howe, Wilson F. Clark, John Wanamaker, and Howard E. Weaver.
>
> While Bryant and Atwood analyzed research and education in the national parks, Prof. J.V.K. Wagar of Colorado A&M State College studied and advocated nature interpretation in forest recreation…
>
> One of the A.I.N.'s first publications was Jean Sanford Replinger's committee report, the "Preparation of the Interpretive Naturalist," which proved useful to colleges. This was followed by the more comprehensive and statistically reliable doctoral study of Benjamin D. Mahaffey at Texas A&M University in 1972.

## The Power of the Written Word

Since the 1950s, a number of authors forged a vocabulary for modern interpretation through their published works. The identification of principles, approaches, and cross-referenced research launched a profession based on the foundation of humankind's natural tendencies to understand their surroundings and keep culture alive from generation to generation.

Freeman Tilden, the son of a newspaper publisher in Boston, chose to travel the world as a young man while his friends attended Ivy League colleges. When he returned to the United States, he pursued his interests in writing and became a

**Freeman Tilden**

skilled author and playwright. His abilities as a writer and editor became well regarded in the publishing community.

In 1954, Alfred A. Knopf personally invited Tilden to write a book on national parks. The resulting book, *National Parks: What they Mean to You and Me*, brought Tilden an invitation by National Parks Director Newton B. Drury to write a book on interpretation with financial support from the Old Dominion Foundation. In 1957 *Interpreting Our Heritage* was released and quickly became an important first text in this growing profession. Tilden's six principles were so well regarded in the field that they are still taught by National Association for Interpretation as a fundamental part of its Certified Interpretive Guide course. The book gives both a historical perspective of the field as well as a firm grounding in basic interpretive principles. Interestingly, many of Tilden's principles seem to reflect the field-tested revelations provided by Enos Mills in earlier writings that included *Adventures of a Nature Guide*.

At age 87, Tilden took a final tour of national parks at the request of the National Park Service to advise them regarding "environmental issues" and what seemed to be working in the field. Tilden's driver, Walt Dabney, was a recent college graduate at the time. Dabney went on to become Director of Texas Parks and Wildlife Department after a long career as a ranger and superintendent at many national parks. In the NPS publication *Interpretation*, Dabney reflected:

> Freeman was 87 and I was 23, the year we spent together. We shared a lot of adventures and discussions, got on each other's nerves at times and became good friends. He loved the Park Service more than any other of his various careers. He really believed in the purpose of the agency and felt its employees had made and could continue to make a "moral" difference in the nation.[28]

During that journey, Tilden sent a memo to NPS Director George Hartzog that framed his beliefs about the power and importance of this new profession.

> . . . to give the word Interpretation a fuller meaning and a greater impact. You say well that we can help to answer the question, "Who Am I?" It can never be answered by knowing the name of a flower or the date of a battle. It can begin by being in contact with the beauty and mystery of nature, and the scene of social struggle. From that contact, inspirational by itself, we must develop the appreciation that does not speak for itself: "What this means in your life." "What are you doing here?" . . . the aim of man to rise above himself, and to choose the option of quality rather than material superfluity.

Grant Sharpe, a professor and departmental chair at University of Washington made an important contribution to the interpretive profession as editor and an author of *Interpreting the Environment*.[29] He brought together many of the most experienced interpretive trainers and teachers of the time to create a teaching resource of great importance at the time. It gave interpretive classes being taught at colleges and universities a quality resource as a text for basic and advanced courses. For agencies and organizations it provided a great library resource and training aid, reflecting the state of the art and science of the time.

Next on the scene was a "from the front lines" manual from William "Bill" Lewis. Lewis began his career as a National Park Service interpreter at Yellowstone National Park in 1949. He was appointed as Yellowstone's "communication specialist" in 1970 and began training the staff of 55 interpreters and seasonal workers at that time. He also trained at Mather and Albright Training Centers for NPS as well as with other agencies throughout the U.S. and Canada. In

GUEST ESSAY

# Grant Sharpe Blazed the Trail
*by Sam Ham*

It is important that all of us in the interpretation field—particularly our younger colleagues who were unable to know Grant W. Sharpe personally—recognize the immense contribution this amazing man has had on us, on what we do, and on the things we care about most in professional life. Few others in the history of parks, protected areas, and interpretation will ever equal his impact. The careers of nearly two generations of interpretation professionals have taken place on Grant's "watch," and there is little doubt that each of us has walked a smoother road laden with more opportunity because of his advocacy and the strong credible voice he brought to interpretation.

**Grant Sharpe**

Grant died peacefully on the morning of January 17, 2006, in Bremerton, Washington. He had just turned 80. His entire family was present at the time of his death. He did not suffer. The official cause of death was liver failure.

Grant Sharpe accomplished more in life than a lot of contemporary interpreters may realize. There will be official obituaries, and many lists of richly deserved accolades will no doubt be published about him. But if I could summarize the significance of this professor's life in a single thought, it would be that he was almost singularly responsible for legitimizing interpretation as a profession as well as a field of study in higher education. He fought battles that none of us who followed would ever have to fight, and he published *Interpreting the Environment*, the first-ever text attempting a scholarly analysis of interpretation, among many other scholarly works. These unparalleled efforts over a 40-year period helped to set the table for interpretation's credibility both in universities around the world and within organizations and institutions that today develop and present interpretive programs. During his life, Grant W. Sharpe nurtured, cultivated, and shaped an entire profession, and virtually anyone who wears the label "interpreter" is indebted in some way to this unusual man. I, like many of his colleagues, feel fortunate simply to have lived when he did. Things would have been so much more difficult had he not blazed the trail in front of us.

*Originally published in* InterpNews, *Spring 2006*

1980 he published *Interpreting for Park Visitors,*[30] an easily read handbook for anyone working in parks or outdoor resource area. Lewis' notion of the "interactive threesome," comprising the audience, the resource, and the interpreter, continues to be taught in diverse programs because it clearly identifies the key components of the profession. Lewis taught at the University of Vermont from 1954 until his retirement, while devoting his summers to Yellowstone National Park.

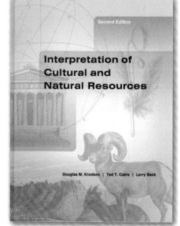

Every field needs a comprehensive text that encapsulates the essence of the profession. Taking on the task for the field of interpretation, Doug Knudson at Purdue University, Larry Beck of San Diego State University and Ted Cable at Kansas State University collaborated in writing *Interpretation of Cultural and Natural Resources.*[31] This textbook for interpretation provides detailed coverage of the theoretical and applied field of heritage interpretation with careful reference to the social science research that underpins the profession.

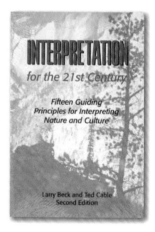

Another comprehensive and user-friendly text made an appearance in 1995 with Sam Ham's *Environmental Interpretation: A Practical Guide for People with Big Ideas and Small Budgets.*[33] Sam Ham began his career working at Kamiak Butte before it became one of Washington's state parks. He completed graduate studies in cognitive psychology and became a faculty professor at University of Idaho. In 1992 his book was published simultaneously in Spanish and English with case histories in each language unique to the cultures most likely to use the book. It quickly became one of the most popular texts at universities as well as a prized possession of Latin American park and protected managers with very limited access to print resources. Its focus on the interpretive approach to communication is very teachable and builds around thematic communication, an idea Sam attributes to his mentor, Bill Lewis. However, in a 2000 *Legacy* magazine interview, Lewis gives the credit for the idea of thematic interpretation to Aristotle.[34]

Tilden's enduring contribution to the profession was a starting point for many other authors. In 1998 Ted Cable and Larry Beck wrote *Interpretation for the 21st Century*[32] as an update to Tilden's book. In this book, the authors provide 15 interpretive principles that reflect modern changes in interpretive communication techniques. Although the first six principles pay homage to Tilden's work, the remaining principles plunge into new territory with history of place, technology, support, and experience design.

Other important texts include the Interpreter's Handbook Series by Mike Gross, Ron Zimmerman, and a variety of co-authors at University of Wisconsin at Stevens Point. Gross and Zimmerman also published *Interpretive Centers*[35] in 2003, providing a comprehensive view of the choices made in diverse settings to create interpretive buildings and programs. In 2002, NAI opened its publishing imprint, InterpPress, with *Personal Interpretation: Connecting Your Audience to Heritage Resources*[36] by Lisa Brochu and Tim Merriman. This book was written as a text for the Certified Interpretive Guide training course to help introduce readers to the variety of resources available to them. In 2003, a new textbook by Lisa Brochu entitled *Interpretive Planning: The 5-M Model for Successful Planning Projects*[37] hit the shelves and has become adopted as a text for a number of college planning

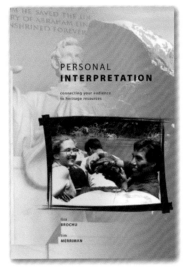

*Personal Interpretation* **is the first book published by NAI's InterpPress**

courses throughout the world. InterpPress publishes one to two titles a year on interpretation-related subjects. 2004 saw the publication of *The Nature Center Book: How to Create and Nurture a Nature Center in Your Community*[38] by Brent Evans and Carolyn Chipman Evans, followed by *Management of Interpretive Sites: Developing Sustainable Operations through Effective Leadership*[39] by Tim Merriman and Lisa Brochu in 2005, and *Interpretive Writing* by Alan Leftridge in 2006.

## Interpretation for the Masses

Books have been important bearers of conservation and interpretive messages for centuries. Many serious scientists took their messages to broader publics by writing books in popular language designed to be more interesting than a simple record of their research or scientific views. Aldo Leopold's *Sand County Almanac*,[40] Rachel Carson's *Silent Spring*[41] and Loren Eiseley's collected essays demonstrate the incredible power of gifted scientists writing for a diverse readership. Margaret Mead popularized anthropology for many readers through her many great books. She inspired countless interpreters who hope they make a difference each day when she said, "Never doubt that a small group of thoughtful, committed people can change the world. Indeed, it is the only thing that ever has."

The list of scientists who interpret their research to broader publics through mass media is admirable. Jacques Cousteau took viewers across and under the seas for wonderful journeys into the unknown while Carl Sagan took readers skyward to better understand the billions of celestial bodies and phenomena in the world of astronomy. Imminent mammalogist George Schaller contacted popular audiences with his books based on his research such as *The Serengeti Lion*,[42] *Stones of Silence*,[43] *The Year of the Gorilla*,[44] and *The Last Panda*.[45] His research on gorillas of the Virunga Volcanoes led to Dian Fosse's research and the movie that popularized her story, "Gorillas in the Mist" (1988). Jane Goodall's chimpanzee research and extraordinary ability to share her work through lectures and documentaries have appealed to wide audiences.

Interpretation for mass audiences has been pioneered by diverse people, but ironically, usually not by people traditionally considered professionals in the interpretation field. The entertainment industry has been a source of interpretive media at least since the 1950s and possibly earlier. Since 1944 the Ad Council, National Association of State Foresters, and USDA Forest Service have collaborated with Smokey Bear messages, media, and memorabilia. The Smokey campaign may well be the longest running public service campaign ever. Though it was devised as an ad campaign, it is also considered "interpretive" because Smokey delivers thematic messages designed to influence human behavior toward stewardship.

With the arrival of television in most homes in the 1950s and 1960s came a new generation of scientists and wildlife enthusiasts. In 1951 Don Herbert, a highly decorated WWII B-24 pilot who flew 56 missions, introduced himself as Mr. Wizard and soon was airing on 91 stations.[46] The National Science Foundation and the American Chemical Society gave the show awards for science education. Mr. Wizard's young assistants helped children connect in new ways to science. Soon, more than 5,000 Mr. Wizard Science Clubs with 100,000 members sprang up around the U.S. The show endured until 1972, but Don Herbert and his wife continued to develop science programs for schools featuring young performers doing children's science experiments. These tours eventually contacted 1.2 million children around the U.S. In 1984, *Discovery* magazine reported that Herbert insisted that his purpose in life was not to teach but to have fun. "I just restrict myself to fun that has scientific content." Though he focused on "gee whiz" experiments to turn kids on to science, the show had emotional hooks largely due to the kid assistants.

BILL NYE, INC.

**Bill Nye the Science Guy**

Bill Nye the Science Guy[47] followed Mr. Wizard's good work with his own unique style of interpreting science in an entertaining way. Meanwhile, on Canadian television an entomologist by the name of John Acorn became the star of an Animal Planet cable show entitled, "Acorn, the Nature Nut."[48] His great skill as a naturalist and ecologist augments the pizzazz of a natural showman who also plays banjo and several other stringed musical instruments, engaging young viewers with his folksy songs. After graduating with two degrees from University of Alberta, Acorn began his career as a park interpreter and later moved into hosting and writing his award winning show. He has authored several children's books, and of this writing, lectures at the University of Alberta, Department of Natural Resources. He also serves as an Associate of the E.H. Strickland Entomology Museum.

Film directors and actors often help mass audiences understand history and important historical figures. Actor/director Sir Richard Attenborough[49] made many films of great power in interpreting history with "Ghandi" (1982) being one of the more memorable. His naturalist brother Sir David Attenborough was also well-respected in media. From Zoo Quest[50] in 1954 to the award-winning Life on Earth[51] series with 500 million viewers, his 50-year career has had great impact. His list of awards from science and media organizations is almost as long as his impressive list of natural and cultural films and shows.

In 1990 Kevin Costner produced and directed an Oscar-wining movie, "Dances with Wolves,"[52] paying homage to the story of the Lakota people in the American West as the U.S. Army began establishing a presence through the late 1800s. Costner was so touched by his experience with the Lakota people and close encounters with bison during the filming of the movie that he purchased and restored property near Deadwood, South Dakota to create an interpretive site known as Tatanka: Story of the Bison, where Lakota people can tell their own stories.

TIM MERRIMAN

**Tatanka: Story of the Bison**

In addition to the wide screen, historical interpretation appeared early on television with no less journalistic talent than Walter Cronkite[53] who hosted "You Are There" from 1953 to 1957. Though it lasted only a few years, the films played over and over again in schools throughout the U.S. during the next two decades. This show laid the groundwork for the diverse programming that can be seen today on the History Channel. Each episode let viewers experience historical events with Cronkite acting as the interpreter to help them understand the significance of the event.

Nature programs emerged as a part of the television scene even earlier. Mutual of Omaha's Wild Kingdom[54] began on a Sunday in January 1963 and often reigned in its time slot until the program ended in 1988. At one point it beat variety shows such as Hee Haw and The Lawrence Welk Show in the ratings. The host of the program, Marlin Perkins, was the director of the Lincoln Park Zoo when he began hosting Zoo Parade on a Chicago station in 1949, after shooting episodes in the basement of the Lincoln Park Zoo Reptile House. Perkins moved to the St. Louis Zoo as director and stayed with Wild Kingdom until his death in 1986. Every week for two and a half decades, he and his assistant Jim Fowler took up to 34 million viewers on a vicarious adventure that often resulted in rough and tumble captures of wild animals for research purposes. The show received some criticism for being more entertainment than education, but many budding interpreters were glued to their TV sets, inspired by every episode. Cable television has created many more niches for naturalists and historians to interpret. Ken Burns[55] has been the most admired documentarian with a diverse portfolio of accomplishments from the award-winning Civil War (1990) series on Public Television to the Oscar-nominated Brooklyn Bridge (1981), Huey Long (1985), The Statue of Liberty (1985), The Congress (1988), Thomas Hart Benton (1988), and Empire of the Air: The Men Who Made Radio (1991).

Television programming opened a new window into the world of interpretation. The 1950s also saw the opening of one of the most well-known theme parks in the world. Although many interpreters seem reluctant to view such venues as interpretive opportunities, the use of thematic material blended with an entertainment component actually created a new concept with great appeal to the masses. Opened in 1955, Disneyland[56] entertained more than 50 million people in its first 10 years. Founder Walt Disney described his hopes for the experience in Frontierland in this statement:

> All of us have a cause to be proud of our country's history, shaped by the pioneering spirit of our forefathers. . . .. Our adventures are designed to give you the feeling of having lived, even for a short while, during our country's pioneer days.

Walt Disney did not live to see his next dream project open in Florida in 1971, but his brother Roy called the new park Walt Disney World (WDW)[57] to honor Disney's creative genius. Disney's built environments engaged the public in a variety of ways, but EPCOT Center[58] took a very definite thematic interpretive direction. Originally designed as the Environmental Prototype Community Of Tomorrow, it endeavored to link interpretation of history, the environment, diverse cultures, technology, and the vast potential of imagination. In the mid-1980s some Disney cast (staff) members became involved in NAI's interpretive training opportunities. By 1990 WDW created a corporate office to manage environmental quality issues. Recycling expanded throughout the park grounds and backstage area and Chip and Dale, the chipmunks, became the recycling mascots with Jiminy Cricket as the environmentality spokesman. The Disney Wilderness Preserve in Kissimmee was purchased by Disney Development Corporation as mitigation for the 30,000 acres developed at WDW, developed and managed through a partnership with The Nature Conservancy. In 1995, CEO Michael Eisner announced the planned 1998 opening of WDW's Animal Kingdom.[59] The entertainment factor remains intact, but conservation is a major theme of the area interpreted through site and facility design, signage, exhibits, and programming.

NAI hosted a national meeting in Orlando in 1995 and went behind the scenes to learn more about Disney's extraordinary customer service. WDW staff members assisted in planning and executing the workshop for more than 1,000 attendees. Almost every major newspaper subsequently carried some variation of the headline "Park Rangers Play at WDW."[60] Congressman Klinger's investigation on government waste demanded federal participants to report on how often they skipped sessions to play in the theme parks. NBC called the NAI office for member phone numbers to do interviews for a "Fleecing of America" story. Resulting investigations found that most NAI professionals attended the educational sessions at the workshop and saw little of the adjacent theme park. NBC dropped their story and the Congressman's office found nothing illegal or unethical in the National Interpreters Workshop at WDW. In 2004 Animal Kingdom hosted a Certified Interpretive Trainer's Workshop backstage, with several WDW staff members in attendance.

WDW reaches an immense and diverse audience. Its conservation messages and interpretive approaches to media are an extension of the good work done at thousands of parks, zoos, museums, nature centers, aquariums, and historic sites and may reach the audiences who would not usually attend more traditional interpretive sites.

Interpretation is a communication process that is not limited to any specific type of venue. The profession can have impact in almost any setting. Reaching mass audiences simply increases the opportunities to deliver important messages about sustainability of heritage resources. It is easy to be a critic of entertaining approaches to interpretation but each opportunity to connect people with resources should be valued. Sea World-San Diego[61] was the brainchild of four UCLA graduates who first thought they would build an underwater restaurant. This initial concept evolved into a 22-acre park that opened in 1964 to 400,000 visitors in its first year. By 1970 Sea World began building other parks in Ohio, Florida, and Texas. Textbook publishers Harcourt, Brace, and Jovanovich owned controlling interest in the Sea World parks from 1976 to 1989. Ownership passed to Anheuser-Busch in 1989 and Busch Entertainment took over management. The triple focus of entertainment, research, and education allows Sea World to engage millions of visitors with a conservation message while they enjoy the marine life displayed at the parks. Conservation messages permeate much of the exhibitry and programs.

Many other mass media have also been effective interpreters through their articles and photos. *National Geographic* has been an important popular publication since it began in 1888.[62] The magazine was created by 33 men who met on Lafayette Square near the White House in Washington, D.C. The long history of reporting stories of research and exploration behind the trademarked yellow frame evolved into the National Geographic Explorer series on cable television. *Audubon Magazine, National Wildlife, Ranger Rick, Orion, Natural History, Smithsonian,* and *Natural History* are just a few publications through the years that have built large readerships beyond the ranks of scientists and historians.

The National Association for Interpretation has published *Legacy* magazine since 1990. In 2005 NAI added *The Interpreter* magazine with the desire to shift the focus of *Legacy* from professional interpreters to the broader audiences of the 500,000 docents and volunteers who interpret for agencies and organizations around the U.S. Mass audiences have become more interested in natural and cultural history through the creative work of legions of people in print and electronic media over the years. Interpretation

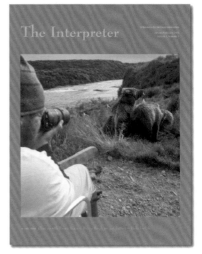

professionals can be found in the agencies and organizations of natural and cultural resources, and also in commercial venues and scientific circles. No matter who employs them, interpreters will continue to find new audiences in the fast-paced world of mass media.

GUEST ESSAY

# The Heritage of Interpretation
*by Jim Covel*

There was a time in this country's not-so-distant past
when we began to come to grips with the future of
America's natural resources. The science of biology was
still primitive, and specialties such as ecology and
wildlife management were concepts yet to be developed.
Still, a few biologists were alarmed with the rate at which our flora and
fauna were vanishing and realized that an attempt must be made to describe
and catalog our natural heritage while the opportunity existed. Thus an
interesting new breed of adventurer appeared which was popularly referred
to as a field "naturalist."

Some of these naturalists were well-educated; many were self-made
students of nature. Their principal objective was to go a field and study or
collect specimens, which represented the native flora and fauna of habitats
throughout the country, with a particular focus on the West, where much of
the plant and animal life was relatively undescribed. The names of some of
these naturalists are memorialized through the names of animals, such as
John James Audubon, Thomas Nuttall, David Douglas, Spencer Baird, and
many others.[63] The ideal collector was a good shot, an able outdoorsman
who could travel in the field for months at a time, could prepare his or her
own specimens, and was willing to live this nomadic life for little personal
gain other than the satisfaction of contributing to our knowledge of our
natural heritage.

As science progressed the mission of the traditional biological survey
teams diminished. Some of the naturalists were relegated to museums where
they continue to work with volumes of material collected by their peers. But
a select few could see a new thirst for knowledge was growing on the part of
the general public. Our society was becoming increasingly urbanized and
isolated from nature. Children and adults wanted to learn about the
wonders of the natural environment and the ways of other creatures that
share this planet with us. Into this growing information gap jumped some
of these field naturalists who were able to popularize the existing scientific
knowledge of the day.

A parallel effort was underway on the cultural history front. As we
matured as a nation we realized the importance of preserving the places,

artifacts and other symbols of the defining moments in our history. As early as the 1790s local and state historical societies were being formed to keep our heritage alive and make it available for future generations. Again, the initial focus was on gathering and recording the data, stories and objects that constitute historic events before they were lost. Professional and amateur historians alike discovered a characteristic common to all interpreters—if you love something, you want to share it with others. Interpreting our cultural heritage through oral tradition grew into more formal lectures and programs as well as written interpretation of historic events.

Growing out of the work of these naturalists and historians, the term interpreter was developed to describe someone who was able to interpret the natural or cultural environment to the public and communicate the significance and meaning of our heritage. This usage of the term may go back over 500 years to Leonardo DaVinci who described himself as an "interpreter" of nature and man through his art.

There is a cadre of nature writers, artists, historians and early conservationists that, in hindsight, would also be viewed as interpreters. Certainly John Muir and Henry David Thoreau helped transform our view of the wilderness from a hostile frontier to a national treasure. William Henry Jackson and Carleton Watkins were some of the first to use the new art of photography to create a national vision of our significant places and people. Aldo Leopold established our sense of stewardship for the land. Theodore Roosevelt, Gifford Pinchot, and Stephen Mather deserve credit for their ability to move a nation to protect its heritage and resources. All of these people had one thing in common—the ability to inspire us, and to create such a strong connection to people and places that we acted to set aside the special resources that define us as a nation. They too are part of the heritage of interpretation.

Women are prominent in the lineage of modern interpreters. Certainly Rachel Carson jumps to mind as the mother of the modern environmental movement, and Anna Botsford Comstock is credited with developing the concept of environmental education in schools. Florence Merriam Bailey, sister of Hart Merriam, played a pivotal role in supporting the fledgling Audubon Society and wrote the *Field Guide to Western North American Birds*, which became a prototype for the later series by Roger Tory Peterson. In northern California where I grew up, Alice Eastwood and Helen Sharsmith were legendary botanists who inspired generations of naturalists.[64] Laurel Reynolds was a housewife with a passion for nature. Her hobby of family photography turned into a serious pursuit of moviemaking, with nature as a new focus. Her film "Island in Time" is credited with swaying public sentiment and political support to create Point Reyes National Seashore.[65]

Another forerunner of the interpreter was a group of people who, for lack of a better term, were referred to simply as guides. These folks had both expertise and passion for a particular place or resource, and shared both of those freely with others that came to explore and discover. They too had that rare ability to connect us to a place, to inspire us through words and experiences, and to convey a sense of heritage and stewardship. Enos Mills was certainly one of the finest examples of this profession, and there were many others who were associated with lodges, parks and cultural sites.

Many interpreters might trace their lineage to early efforts in the national parks and forest preserves where one role assigned to the multi-purpose rangers, wardens, and gamekeepers was to greet the public and open their eyes to the wonders of these sites. Galen Clark was designated as an official "Guardian of Yosemite" in 1866. Civil War veteran Harry Yount was appointed the official gamekeeper of Yellowstone Park in 1880, even before the military became active in the park in 1886.[66] Over the next 20 years, the nation's parks and forest reserves were guarded by a combination of military troops and civilian appointees when the troops were unavailable, and their duties often included playing the host or hostess to a growing number of visitors. In 1898 Congress appropriated funds to pay civilian "special forest agents" who eventually became known as "forest rangers." By 1916 when the National Park Service was formally designated, there were rangers in at

"Guardian of Yosemite" Galen Clark in front of the Grizzly Giant Tree, Mariposa Grove, Yosemite National Park around 1858-1859.

least nine national parks.[67] Soon park rangers would become as much a part of American culture as the National Parks themselves. These early rangers were the original jack- or jill-of-all-trades. However, as seasonal visitation grew in parks, the practice of adding special programs delivered by seasonal rangers grew common starting in the 1920s. In addition, there was a growing demand to interpret the natural and cultural history of park sites, and these early interpretive programs had a heavy academic flavor to them. Often college students and faculty were recruited for these seasonal positions. In 1919 Dr. Harold Bryant and Dr. Loye Miller were hired to conduct summer "nature walks and evening lectures" for visitors to

Yosemite.[68] Other parks soon followed suit and many larger parks would add a permanent ranger-naturalist or ranger-historian who served as the resident expert on park resources and trained/supervised additional seasonal staff, often referred to as "90-day wonders."

Nature and history programs surged again after the end of WWII as the American public experienced a renewed interest in travel and exploring our heritage. By that time many states had well-established park systems that included rangers who delivered a variety of interpretive programs. Municipal park systems in Oakland, California, and Cleveland, Ohio, were among the first to institute interpretive naturalist programs at the local level in the 1940s.

Things have come full circle, as all things do in nature, and again we have become increasingly concerned with the rapid loss of critical resources and natural areas, the same concerns that spawned the first naturalists and historians over 150 years ago. The special talents of today's interpreters are now being brought to bear in saving parklands, critical habitats, and other significant natural and cultural resources—those things that make our lives not only possible but also meaningful.

# 4

# THE BIRTH OF A PROFESSIONAL ORGANIZATION

The National Association for Interpretation (NAI) officially became a nonprofit organization with the U.S. Internal Revenue Service on August 29, 1989, but that act alone does not accurately explain how this important professional association began a half century or more ago. Over a period of several years, two parent organizations moved toward consolidation through a fairly complicated process to become what is now known as NAI.

The beginning of it all is difficult to define. Does an organization begin with discussions about the need for professionals to meet regularly, the actual first meeting of such a group, the first election of officers, or the IRS designation as a 501(c)3 nonprofit association? NAI leaders have generally decided that the decision to get together each year signified the organization's beginnings. That important choice made by early members greatly pre-dated the various official acts recorded on government paperwork.

## Association of Interpretive Naturalists (AIN)

In the 1950s, the Great Lakes Parks Training Institute (GLPTI) regularly convened an annual meeting. This rich combination of professional networking and socializing was held at Pokagon State Park in northern Indiana. It attracted a variety of park professionals from Illinois, Indiana, Michigan, Ohio, and a few other surrounding states and, as of this writing, continues to meet annually. A group of  naturalists who worked with metropolitan park districts was especially keen to convene its own meeting. In 1954, they agreed to have their first naturalist conclave the following year at Bradford Woods, an outdoor education center for University of Indiana. From then on, these founding members met annually separate from GLPTI, initiating their own special network of colleagues, eager to share their frustrations and successes. Bradford Woods continued to provide a

**Early AIN meetings took place in Bradford Woods in Indiana.**

spiritual home for this informal network for many years. A decade passed and the meetings became more valued by the participants, leading to discussions of formalizing an organization.

Structure came slowly, but in 1958 Robert Kelly of DuPage County Forest Preserves in Illinois suggested that the time had come to create a formal organization. A steering committee chaired by Howard Weaver and composed of Kenny Dale, William Hopkins, Roland Eisenbeis, William Price, Alan Helmsley, Walter Tucker, and Robert Kelly met April 3-5 at Bradford Woods to initiate a process. In 1961 the group elected Harold Wallin of Cleveland Metroparks as president and Howard Weaver as vice-president. Robert Kelly became secretary-treasurer and John Kason headed the membership committee. The other steering committee members served on the first board of directors.[69]

Charles M. Goethe was named the first honorary member of AIN for his philanthropy in conservation and foresight in bringing the nature guide idea to Yosemite National Park after observing programs at Switzerland's "Lake of the Four Forest Canions." Freeman Tilden became the second honorary member in 1963 in recognition of his contributions to the field through his publications about interpretation in the national parks. A professional code of ethics policy was presented in 1962 at a meeting at Glen Helen, a facility of Antioch College, in Yellow Springs, Ohio. In 1964 the revised code of ethics was officially adopted. Dr. Howard "Howdy" Weaver at University of Illinois filed papers in 1965 to create an

Illinois nonprofit corporation with a 501(c)3 Internal Revenue Service designation using the name of the Association of Interpretive Naturalists (AIN). Consequently, AIN seemed to originate in Illinois because the IRS tax-exempt ruling letter and articles of incorporation were filed in that state, despite its longer history of informal meetings in Indiana.

Membership in AIN grew slowly and steadily to over 600 by 1974. Maryland Capital Parks and Planning Commission (MCPPC) in Derwood, Maryland, offered AIN free office space. The growth in numbers of AIN members made it necessary to hire a paid staff member to manage membership records. Peggy Van Ness became the first office manager for AIN in 1975.

Members of AIN in its first two decades tended to be interpretive naturalists, recreation planners, and managers of natural history programs. AIN required that a prospective member get the signatures of three existing professional members to qualify for membership. Students could join the organization but were not allowed to vote until they became professional members. AIN continued to grow steadily until it had almost 1,000 members by 1985.

AIN's constitution allowed the formation of sub-units based upon geographic proximity. Members in ten areas across the United States submitted petitions to the board of directors to request recognition as regional units of AIN. The numbering system for regions was based on the order in which the region became recognized, so the southwest became Region 1, since it was first to petition the board of directors. Regional workshops and newsletters became important networking services that bound together these fledgling groups. Eventually, each state and some provinces in Canada had a regional home, allowing regional directors to become the logical choices for serving on the national board of directors as representatives of the members within their geographic region.

### Western Interpreters Association (WIA)

In an audiotape[70] provided to NAI as background on the Western Interpreters Association, Chris Nelson tells the story of Bill Knott coming to the Sacramento Junior Museum, where Chris served as executive director, to invite him to join his staff at the Oakland Parks and Recreation Department and East Bay Regional Park District. Chris moved from Sacramento to the East Bay area to work in this unique parks program. Bill Knott believed interpretation was a core role of their staff. At about that same time the California State Park Rangers formed a subgroup known as the California State Park Naturalists Association.

As chief of interpretation at East Bay Regional Park District, Chris Nelson supported the group but recognized that the group provided virtually no services for the dues collected. Budget problems and the widely dispersed interpreters in the state system in California made it difficult for the fledgling California State

**WIA was officially formed during this meeting at Tilden Regional Park in Berkeley, California, in 1969, when Chris Nelson was elected president.**

Park Naturalists Association to function as an organization. Facing dues competition with the well-established California State Park Rangers Association, the naturalists subgroup was not destined to survive.

East Bay Regional Park staff organized a meeting of about 20 interpreters at Folsom Dam in 1968 to talk about the need for a more specialized interpreters group in the western United States. Chris related, "I think at that time AIN probably had about eight paid members west of the Rocky Mountains. I think most of those were on my staff. And the feeling that we should also be doing something, or that we should maybe become an AIN chapter, took hold."

They agreed to form an organization called Western Park Interpreters Association (WPIA) at the Folsom meeting with Darwin Thorpe as president. A year later the name was changed to Western Interpreters Association during a meeting at Tilden Nature Area and Chris Nelson was elected as president. They started *The Interpreter* as a newsletter and began to investigate chapter status with AIN in hopes of one day merging the organization with AIN. Chris was also elected to the AIN board of directors and served as vice-president from 1975 to 1977. Bill Knott supported Chris' many trips east to AIN board meetings due to his belief in the importance of interpretation to their park system.

WIA's birth led to a growing membership in California and along the west coast. The organization grew to 120 members by 1973 when the distinctive logo was adopted depicting half a wagon wheel with the circle completed by the branches of a tree, showing both natural and cultural roots. *The Interpreter* became a well-respected publication under the editorial expertise of Alan Leftridge and attracted many AIN members to join WIA. Still nurturing the idea of merging AIN and WIA, the boards of each organization agreed to a joint meeting at Asilomar Conference Grounds in Pacific Grove, California, in 1974. Hopes were dashed as the two boards discussed how a merger might occur, as each group now had a significant investment in its own ways of conducting business. Membership in WIA had grown to 344 in that same year with students being one-third of the membership.

WIA was particularly successful in creating chapters based on localized geographic areas. California had the Bay Area, Sacramento, Sierra-San Joaquin, Fire Mountains, Southern Cal, San Diego-Border, and North Coast Chapters by the mid-1980s. Chapters proliferated in other parts of the country and by 1986 included Oregon, Utah, National Capital, Nevada, Centennial (Colorado), Oklahoma-Texas, Arizona, Midwest, and Oklahoma. Chapter presidents served on WIA's board of directors, but with 80 percent of its members in California, the single state carried much of the responsibility for the organization's growth and management. Chapter workshops and newsletters, like the regional services with AIN, were important services for members and aided in growing the organization. Doug Bryce became the organization's executive manager, a role he also held with the California Park Rangers Association, to maintain membership records and assist the board with service delivery.

## A Move to Consolidate

With two professional associations for interpreters, dual memberships began to emerge. By 1984, each organization had about 1000 members, and about 100 people held memberships in both organizations. Serious consideration of consolidating AIN and WIA into one stronger organization emerged as early as 1971. Several joint national meetings and joint board meetings encouraged collaboration between the groups. WIA had *The Interpreter* magazine, a themed periodical featuring amusing illustrations by Keith Hoofnagle and his diminutive cartoon rangers known as rangeroons.

AIN published a monthly newsletter and the peer-refereed *Journal of Interpretation*, which provided support for the growing number of serious research articles in the profession. Each organization held annual national meetings with additional meetings of its respective subunits of regions or chapters. Dual members valued the increasingly diverse services of the two organizations and often found the occasional joint meeting even more interesting than those held separately.

As early discussions of consolidation continued, it became clear that AIN leadership would not change the name of the organization, even though a substantial number of its members whose interests went beyond natural history were urging consideration of a more inclusive title. Meanwhile, more than half of WIA's members were cultural history interpreters who found the "naturalist" identity inappropriate. A high percentage of WIA members were students who had a vote in association business, but students were denied the right to vote in AIN. AIN required references from three professional members to gain entry to the organization and WIA had no similar requirement. These and other personal leadership differences caused discussions of a consolidation to break down at Asilomar and a series of successive meetings over the next decade. It seemed the profession was destined to have two competing organizations vying for the same members, while those individuals who wanted the services and networking opportunities of each organization would continue to pay twice for the privilege.

About 90 percent of WIA's membership worked in California, Oregon, and Washington, with the remaining 10 percent scattered over the country. AIN members were more abundant east of the Rocky Mountains. In many ways, the two organizations seemed like they had widely divergent audiences and interests and a few vocal members of each promoted that perception. But a survey of both groups by Lisa Brochu in 1985 indicated that most members saw more similarities than differences and did not oppose consolidation, but favored it. The results of that study led AIN President Tim Merriman and WIA President Alan Kaplan to meet at the First World Heritage Congress in Banff, Alberta, in 1985. Their conversations led to the 1986 appointment of three persons from each organization to explore the implications and logistics of consolidation. At the same time, planning for a joint AIN/WIA workshop to be held in St. Louis, Missouri was undertaken. As part of that effort, program chair Lisa Brochu set up a meeting with chiefs of interpretation for several federal agencies in an effort to determine how to get more federal involvement in the upcoming joint workshop. Dave Dame from National Park Service, Jerry Coutant from USDA Forest Service, George Tabb from US Army Corps of Engineers, and James Massey from US Fish and Wildlife Service met for the first time as a group in the Library of Congress cafeteria. The historic meeting, facilitated by Brochu, was well-received as the potential emerged for learning about each other's operations and working together on a variety of projects. The group, which became known as the Federal Interagency Council on Interpretation, continued to meet quarterly and expanded over the next 20 years to include representatives from NAI, NASA, NOAA, US Environmental Protection Agency, and US Geological Survey.

# The Western Interpreters Association
*by Chris Nelson*

In 1962, William Penn Mott, Jr. ("Mr. Parks") walked into the Sacramento Junior Museum where I was the executive director. Mr. Mott had just been hired to breathe new life into the East Bay Regional Park District, headquartered in Oakland California. One of his primary goals was to make interpretation a key focus in this burgeoning park system. My life was changed forever when I was hired to create a new interpretive department, at department head level.

About two years into my new job it became apparent that there was no organization that could bring all interpreters together to learn and to share. I joined AIN to lay the groundwork for those of us in the west to join that organization.

I found out that the California state park system had a small group of "ranger-interpreters" who had tried to create an organization. I contacted key people in that group, only to find out that their organization never got off the ground. They were invited to meet with me, my staff and other local professional interpreters. Out of that meeting the Western Interpreters Association (WIA) was born. I was elected to be the first president.

The initial roster consisted of 12 members, six of whom were on my staff. Following that first meeting, nature centers and parks throughout the west hosted get-togethers and field trip explorations.

There was a need to create a newsletter and a brochure to promote our association. The first copy of *The Interpreter* was produced by my staff, and a first-run of 25 copies was drafted and mimeographed. The adventures of "Captain Ecology" lent a touch of humor to the text.

During my attendance at an AIN conference, I met with the officers to discuss what we might do to bring the two organizations closer together. Although some of the original differences were still a barrier, I offered to host a national conference with contributions from both organizations.

I chose the famous Asilomar conference center in Pacific Grove, on the California coast. Next-door was Carmel and Point Lobos State Park, often called "the greatest meeting of the land and the sea." We attracted a crowd. One of the eastern attendees took his camera out, and we never saw him again!

Membership in WIA was slowly growing, but it was hard to find officers to serve. One president was finally convinced to serve after a few of us worked him over in a topless bar!

In 1988 history was made, as you all know, when AIN and WIA joined forces to create NAI setting in motion one of the most successful professional organizations, for its size, anywhere.

GUEST ESSAY

# Influences
*by Cem Basman*

When considering the better interpreters I have
encountered over the years, the name Neil Coen always
finds itself in the forefront of my memories. Neil would
spend his summers as a seasonal interpreter at Rocky
Mountain National Park in Colorado. During the
remainder of the year, he was a high school teacher in Kansas City,
Missouri. He was an extraordinary interpreter exemplifying all the traits
that made him stand out among his peers. He was articulate, charismatic,
knowledgeable, and authentic in his enthusiasm. When his schedule
permitted, I would ask Neil to come and speak to the interpretation class I
taught at Colorado State University. His definition of the qualities that
identify a good interpreter has always stuck with me—and has become a
staple component of my training of future interpreters. It was simple. Neil
said that good interpretation must always achieve two things: First, the
interpreter must always tell the truth without exception. And second, always
tell a story. It was so simple—so unequivocal.

When I was asked to write this essay about my experiences and
observations regarding the founding of the National Association for
Interpretation from the perspective of one of its parent organizations, the
Association of Interpretive Naturalists, I thought of Neil Coen's identifiers
of good interpretation and decided to tell a true story about the evolution
of our professional organization. Actually, they are the stories of four people
who may have had the most important influence on the history of NAI and
hence, the history of the interpretive profession.

First is the story of Rey Carlson. The earlier years of the creation
and evolution of the Association of Interpretive Naturalists were
influenced by a cadre of dedicated and motivated individuals. These
pioneers of the interpretation profession are to be revered and honored.
The one name that unmistakably enters any discussion or stories relating
to AIN inevitably is Rey Carlson. Telling the complete story of the
Carlson influence on the interpretation profession may require several
volumes—so rich is this one individual's print on the profession. He has
been identified as the single most influential force behind the founding
of AIN at Bradford Woods in Indiana. Many sources account Rey as

providing the original concept of having a professional organization for interpretive naturalists.

This charming, nurturing, and talented man has directly influenced many individuals in the field of interpretation. In 1977, Rey gave sage counsel to a young man who had just discovered the field of interpretation and was considering pursuing it as a career. I am forever grateful for having had that serendipitous conversation with Rey Carlson. Today, finding myself teaching interpretation in the same hallways of Indiana University in which Rey Carlson practiced his magic is most humbling.

There are many anecdotal, almost mythical accounts recalled from the memory of interpreters of the Carlson influence shaping of our profession. However, there are very few recorded accounts of actual events of the Carlson era in the history of AIN. Recent efforts to determine the specific historical accounting of Rey Carlson's influence on interpretation have produced a myriad of oft-conflicting and fuzzy, second-hand memories. While the essence and quintessence of the Carlson story has survived, the first-hand detail may have been lost.

The story of Rey Carlson has taught us a lesson. Regardless of the magnitude of an individual's gifted and dedicated service, not recording the specifics of an event or an era may cause the true accounting of the story to dwell in future debate. I will use this opportunity to unequivocally capture and set the record of the formation of NAI. In my view, the honest history of the formation of NAI from the ranks of AIN can be accounted for by telling of the stories of three people.

To understand the context in which these stories are to be exhibited, one must understand the culture and condition of the interpretive profession prior to NAI. In the ranks of interpreters, there was a growing concern about having two major organizations that provided professional services for interpreters. The Association of Interpretive Naturalists and the Western Interpreters Association were both valuable, providing services that were differentiated enough that joining only one organization did not allow the full gamut of professional services that were available. Many of us were members of both organizations, wondering why we were not represented by a single stronger association.

In 1981, a joint AIN-WIA national workshop in Estes Park, Colorado, provided a fertile ground for a growing voice among the members to question the duality of our professional representation. The ever-growing discontented comments about the need for a merger eventually caused the AIN board of directors to bring the issue of a potential AIN-WIA merger for discussion and action during the 1984 AIN workshop in Calloway Gardens, Georgia. Citing the "great number of members" who were against the consolidation of the organizations, the AIN board seemed disinclined to pursue serious discussions about merger with WIA.

As an advocate for the merger, I found myself feeling angry, dejected, and powerless along with other fellow seekers of a seemingly logical AIN-WIA organizational merger. Yet we were not about to acquiesce to that seemingly unwise decision by the AIN board to refrain form exploring the possibility of a merger. We wondered what action to pursue to empower us to make the creation of a new organization a reality. The simple wisdom that cut the Gordian knot of the consolidation question is best told by the story of another individual.

I vividly recall approaching Tom Christensen at the Calloway Gardens to repeat the concern I had shared with many other colleagues that morning. In his usual adroit and buoyant manner Tom had the answer. He cheerfully expressed the simple need to approach this issue from two points. First, a grassroots effort would be needed to make the changes occur. He suggested that those of us in favor of the merger ought to consider running for leadership roles in the organization to directly influence the decision-making process. Additionally, he pointed out the need to have an accurate accounting of the true desires of the membership regarding the merger. He asked if we really knew what the membership was thinking?

Tom's assessment of the necessities of the moment was quite prescient. Accomplishing the tasks of both of his suggestions would make the merger finally happen in 1988. Perhaps the need for a grassroots movement to converge on the leadership roles of AIN could have been identified by anyone else, but it was Tom who clearly and initially identified the simple, necessary plan to take control of the future of our profession and professional organization. While seldom told, the story of Tom Christensen's grassroots approach that became the call to action of those disenchanted with the lack of action by the board of directors must be recorded.

Along with Tom, many of us pursued and found ourselves in leadership roles on the AIN board of directors. This participatory activity however was not enough to precipitate the merger of the two organizations. An irrefragable and empirical evidence of a majority desire to merge by the interpretation professionals had to be provided. The story of Lisa Brochu's significant role in the consolidation of AIN and WIA is indisputable.

Perhaps conducting the most important survey of the membership in the existing history of the interpretation profession, the young and rising star of the interpretive profession provided the verification necessary to clear the way for the establishment of the new organization, NAI. Lisa asked that very simple question to the membership. The resounding answer was "yes, we do want to have a single voice representing our profession." Lisa was able to categorically show that the persistent and boisterous voices against the consolidation of AIN and WIA were indeed a very small minority. Without Lisa's survey of the members' desires, the question of justifying a merger would have fomented for years. Lisa legitimized and justified the need for the new organization. This single action paved a direct route to the formation of our current professional association.

Having put the supporters of an organizational merger in decision-making roles, and having established an empirical proof of the desire of the members to create a new organization, there remained a need to find the leader to take the helm of this growing movement. This leadership role could not be provided by just anyone. This individual had to have a unique mix of qualities. The leader had to be highly charismatic, articulate, persistent, reconciliatory, motivational, aggressive, accommodating, menacing, creative, professional, compromising, and energetic. Most of all, this leader had to exhibit impeccable professional and personal integrity—enter Tim Merriman. As the final president of AIN, the true story of Tim's role in the establishment of NAI ought never be lost nor diminished. Working at the Greenway and Nature Center of Pueblo with Tim during this time of the organizational growth, I was privileged to have first-hand view of his achievements. Due to his persistence and encouragement, he was the primary motivation for staying on the task of establishing the new organization. Additionally, Tim's creative problem-solving skills were often called upon during this rather pragmatic period of the organizational history.

Those of us who assumed leadership roles in various capacities and regions of the United States knew the need for an overall leader to energize the movement to create a better professional organization for the field of interpretation. Tim Merriman's role in the creation of NAI cannot be marginalized. Perhaps there may have been another leader who could have handled the sometime restive board of directors and a nervous membership. I certainly cannot think of anyone else that could have provided the complex collection of skills necessary to maintain the momentum to complete the task of consolidation. While this essay is not the medium to achieve this task, a detailed accounting of the AIN board of directors, and Tim Merriman's activities should be chronicled and recorded for the institutional history of AIN-WIA-NAI.

In the end, a great number of individuals have had a significant influence on the formation of NAI. Individuals played roles of varying degrees of impact with some people having more of an influence than others. Ideally, all stories ought to be researched and recorded in order to formalize and honor our history. This essay has focused on the service of four different individuals that served a critical role in the institutional heritage of the profession of interpretation. Rey Carlson was the undisputed force behind the development of a professional organization for interpretation. Unfortunately, not having recorded the details of his story has provided us with a critical lesson about the importance of recording our history. Tom Christensen's call for a grassroots movement for a change, Lisa Brochu's empirical evidence for the need to change, and Tim Merriman's unimpeachable leadership skills must be duly recorded.

The story of the forming of our professional organization is one of endurance, dedication, and triumph. In my opinion, these four individuals are among many that have played a significant role in the history of AIN-WIA-NAI. Neil Coen has always been correct. We must capture, record, and tell the true story to interpret our institutional heritage.

# 5

## THE NATIONAL ASSOCIATION FOR INTERPRETATION

### Consolidation Becomes Reality

The National Association for Interpretation (NAI) was designed by the six committee members appointed in 1985 by Tim Merriman and Alan Kaplan. Ann Wright, Rich Koopman, and Tom Christensen of AIN, and Jim Tuck, Donna Pozzi, and Dave Vincent of WIA met several times through 1986–87 to consider the possibility of consolidation and develop a plan that satisfied the boards of directors and the members of both organizations. One of several controversial issues was the location of a new national office. An offer of free office space at the Natural Resources Recreation and Tourism

Department of Colorado State University in Fort Collins provided an appealing option that allowed a compromise between the extreme eastern and western locations of the organizations' previous office spaces. A joint workshop in St. Louis in 1987 was the final meeting of each of the separate organizations. As of January 1, 1988, the National Association of Interpretation was born. In its first year the name was changed to the National Association *for* Interpretation to reflect a more grammatically correct title.

Each of the parent organizations' names focused on members, whether naturalists or interpreters. The consolidation committee agreed that the new organization should be devoted to advancing the profession of interpretation rather than the individual interests of any single member or member group. The shift in focus became an important benchmark for future decision-making by the board of directors.

Although the new organization honored memberships from the parent groups, about 300 members were designated "Founders" of NAI by donating $150 each to the new organization to provide seed money for the move to Colorado

**NAI founders were recognized at the last joint meeting of AIN and WIA, the 1987 National Interpreters Workshop in Saint Louis, Missouri.**

and continuing services. A group photo taken at the St. Louis workshop in 1987 and Founders Plaque documented the origins of the newly consolidated organization. NAI quickly grew to 2,300 members by 1990 as members from each parent group attracted new members. The dreams of an interpretive network voiced at Pokagon State Park in Indiana at the Great Lakes Park Training Institute in 1954 had eventually grown into an expanding network of interpretive professionals under the banner of the National Association for Interpretation.

### NAI's Mission, Vision, and Core Values

The mission of NAI was established as: "Inspiring leadership and excellence to advance natural and cultural interpretation as a profession."

This mission statement endured until 2002 when the board of directors changed it slightly to state: "Inspiring leadership and excellence to advance heritage interpretation as a profession." This change recognized the global use of the term "heritage" to refer to both natural and cultural history.

The vision of the organization, determined through a strategic planning process facilitated by Dr. Corky McReynolds of University of Wisconsin-Stevens Point Treehaven Institute in 1996, was "to become the internationally recognized voice of interpretation." The board later removed the word "internationally" from the vision statement, not because it wished to ignore the intent to become known internationally, but because grammatically, it was redundant.

Strategic planning also defined core values of NAI. These tenets provided guidance for development of products, programs, and services.

"We believe that interpretation is important in accomplishing the missions of our members' organizations." Too often interpretation has been used as entertainment alone, when well-designed programs and products could also achieve management objectives. Consequently interpretive services often get cut back or eliminated during economic recessions. The missions of most resource management organizations often include words such as appreciation, understanding, or stewardship. Interpretation serves a vital purpose in achieving missions that require involvement of the audience. This focus on purpose became an important part of NAI's certification training programs. By 2004 logic models entered the training curriculum, encouraging interpreters to provide objectives that measure their efforts in terms of outputs, outcomes, and impacts. Interpretation becomes more sustainable as the results become more measurable and practitioners plug into the goals and objectives of managers.

"We believe that professional development builds stronger organizations and more capable professionals." NAI, like most professional associations, attempts to build a stronger profession by raising the performance standards for all practitioners. The varied programs, publications, and credentialing by NAI are directed toward this core value.

"We value the biodiversity and cultural diversity of the planet." Usually the mission of an interpretive agency identifies a stewardship component related to biodiversity, cultural diversity, or both. NAI members are committed to protecting and preserving the diverse species of the planet along with its many cultures.

"We connect people with their cultural and natural heritage to promote stewardship of resources." Social marketing is now regarded as one of the more important roles of interpretive services. Building awareness of the resource, encouraging understanding and appreciation, and recruiting people as active stewards usually aligns with the mission, goals, and objectives of the interpreter's organization.

"We believe that interpretation is a communication process that forges emotional and intellectual connections between the interests of the audience and inherent meanings in the resource." This definition of interpretation embraced by NAI is somewhat different from definitions used by Tilden and many other writers over the years. It places the focus on the process of communication rather than the content and emphasizes that both emotional and intellectual connections are desirable. It also recognizes the value of audience assessment in making those connections.

## A Changing Organization

With the consolidation of AIN and WIA, NAI had to address the issue of which products, programs, and services to bring forward and which to leave behind. *The Interpreter* and the *Journal of Interpretation* merged to become *Legacy*, the magazine of the new organization that included both peer-juried research and popular articles. Although peer review of all articles for *Legacy* persisted, researchers found it an unsatisfactory venue for publishing their work. It was not until 1996 that the *Journal of Interpretation Research* was revived as an opportunity for peer-juried research to achieve the required status necessary for academicians to publish their findings. As the profession and the organization continue to evolve, the publications also evolve. In 2005, *The Interpreter* was revived as the in-house member magazine focusing on tools of the trade for interpreters, while *Legacy* now reaches a broader audience through the use of professional quality photography and writing related to interpretive sites, events, and individuals of note. NAI began paying for articles and photos in *Legacy* in 2004.

Both the regional structure of AIN and chapter structure of WIA endured, with the idea that chapters would report to the region in which each resided. The new NAI board of directors comprised 10 regional directors and an executive committee of president, vice-president, secretary, and treasurer elected from the general membership. In 1990, the vice-president role was split into two positions, vice president for administration and vice president for programs, to handle the growing responsibilities that came with growing membership.

Also in 1990, a new subunit that recognized the desire for special interests to network together made an appearance with the Resource Interpretation and Heritage Tourism section. Sections rapidly became an integral part of NAI's structure, with special-interest groups developing in 11 areas by 2005, ranging from the African-American Experience to Zoos, Wildlife Parks, and Aquaria. Section leaders developed the Section Leadership Council in 2002 to encourage dialogue between sections, help sections plan their long-range goals, and elect representatives to serve on the national board of directors.

By 2003, section leaders initiated discussions about how to ensure representation of their interests equal to that of the regions on the national board. This discussion stimulated a review of the implications for reorganizing the board. After a member survey indicated that board reorganization might be desirable, a strategic planning process was initiated to investigate options that might help NAI's board become more efficient and effective. In 2004, a new board structure was approved by the membership to become effective January 1, 2006. The new board would include the five-member executive committee elected by the general membership, four representatives elected from a newly formed Regional Leadership Council, four representatives elected from the Section Leadership Council, and three at-large representatives recommended by the president and approved by the board. Enos Mills wrote in his 1920 book, *Adventures of a Nature Guide*, "may the tribe increase."[71] By 2004, 50 years after the first discussions, NAI had almost 5,000 members throughout the United States and in 32 other countries. Clearly, the tribe was increasing, but more than that, it was evolving into an organization that operated in a business-like fashion to provide support to the profession.

## NAI Programs, Products, and Services

From 1988 to 1995, NAI's office staff consisted of an executive director and an office assistant, with part-time student help as needed. For that entire time, the organization remained housed on the Colorado State University campus in a single office, quickly outgrowing the available space.

In 1995, when Tim Merriman became executive director, the organization began to look for a new home in Fort Collins to accommodate anticipated growth. A 900-square-foot Victorian house one block from the Colorado State University became the organization's first real property. From 1995 to 2003, NAI's membership grew from 2,300 to 4,000, and its professional staff grew to eight full-time and four part-time workers, necessitating another move to larger space. After an exhaustive search in and around Fort Collins, a year-long planning and construction project recycled a former one-story auto repair shop at 230 Cherry Street into a new 8,400-square-foot, two-story office building, library, and training center that opened its doors on June 25, 2004, ready to house the professional staff of 10 full-time and six part-time employees, with room for growth over a 10-year period.

At the time of this writing, NAI's programs, products, and services had grown to include:

- *Legacy* Magazine (six issues per year)
- *The Interpreter* Magazine (six issues per year)
- *Journal of Interpretation Research* (two issues per year)
- *InterpNews* (printed newsletter , four issues per year)
- "Interpretunities" (jobs newsletter, 26 issues per year)
- InterpNet (web site)
- InterpPress (publishes two to three titles per year)
- "NAI Now" (monthly e-mail news announcements)
- Annual Interpretive Management Institute
- Annual National Interpreters Workshop and Trade Show
- Annual Interpreting World Heritage Conference
- Regional/Sectional Newsletters
- Regional/Sectional Workshops
- Media Awards Program
- Scholarship Program
- International Volunteer Program
- Annual International Ecotour
- Certification Courses and Credentials (six categories)

NAI's headquarters in Fort Collins, Colorado, moved from a 900-square-foot Victorian house (right) to a new 8,400-square-foot, two-story office building, library, and training center (above) in 2004.

- Heritage Library and Resource Center
- Association Store (logo clothing items and books)
- International Training Center
- Professional Awards Program

Programs, products, and services are constantly reviewed and improved or new ones developed to meet the growing needs of the profession. Information about all of NAI's most current activities can be found at www.interpnet.com.

## Other Professional Associations

NAI is not the only professional association available to interpreters. Around the world, other organizations provide a variety of valuable products and services.

NAI's Interpreting World Heritage conference creates an opportunity for members of these and other organizations to communicate and discuss issues of local and global importance.

*Association for Heritage Interpretation (AHI)*
The Association for Heritage Interpretation[72] in the United Kingdom describes its purpose as being "for anyone interested in interpretation: the art of helping people explore and appreciate our world. AHI aims to promote high standards in the provision of interpretation and to gain wider recognition of interpretation as a professional activity. The association was founded in 1975 as the Society for the Interpretation of Britain's Heritage."

AHI publishes a journal three times a year on current thinking and practice, and brings members together regularly for workshops, networking and awards. More information is available at www.heritageinterpretation.org.uk.

*Asociación para la Interpretación del Patrimonio (AIP)*
Spain's professional network is the Association for Heritage Interpretation, which translates to much the same name as the group in the United Kingdom, but it is a separate entity with its own active membership. The purpose of AIP[73] is to promote professional recognition of heritage interpretation and its practices, provide support for programs that specialize in interpretation, and publish texts and interpretation-related documents.

*Interpretation Association of Australia (IAA)*
Australia has a very active professional community that includes academics, agency employees, non-governmental organizations, and private for-profit sector businesses, much the same as in the United States. The IAA[74] web site www.interpretationaustralia.asn.au describes the network as "a national membership-based organization dedicated to the advancement of the profession of heritage interpretation. IAA was formed in 1992 to share issues and ideas, improve professional standards and raise the profile of heritage interpretation as a profession. It currently serves more than 400 members in Australia, New Zealand and other countries." In 1996 it served as host to the last World Heritage Interpretation Congress held at the Quarantine Station on Sydney Harbor.

Savannah Guides is a network of interpretive guides in northern Australia that describes itself as "a network of professional tour guides with a collective in-depth knowledge of the natural and cultural assets of the tropical savannahs of northern Australia."

*Interpretation Canada (IC)*
Since 1973 Interpretation Canada[75] has provided services to members across Canada and from a variety of other countries. With 500 members from diverse

organizations IC pursues its "ultimate goal . . . to enhance the development of theory and practice in our field."

IC places an emphasis on peer learning, training, and the sharing of knowledge and skills in informal ways. Its stated definition, adopted in 1976, is:

> Any communication process designed to reveal meanings and relationships of cultural and natural heritage to the public, through first-hand involvement with an object, artifact, landscape, or site.

More information about IC's activities is available at www.interpcan.ca/about.html.

*Interpret Europe*
Interpret Europe[76] "is an international network of individuals dealing with the interpretation of Europe's environmental and cultural heritage. The network was set up in year 2000 as an informal coordination body in order to support and initiate interpretive activities Europe-wide."

GUEST ESSAY

# A Giant Leap Forward for the Profession
*by Sarah D. Blodgett*

The certification program is one of NAI's greatest contributions to the profession of interpretation. It not only recognizes those with existing skills and abilities in the field, but is training front-line interpreters, managers, trainers, and planners to deliver excellent interpretive services using the best interpretive methods available.

For years members debated the merits of certification and what shape the program could take. I remember attending a session in 1994 at the National Interpreters Workshop facilitated by Dr. Gail Vander Stoep during which many opinions were expressed, but there was no clear idea of how to develop and launch a program. This discussion had been going on for many years and involved many committees over the years. Feeling frustrated, one member told Lisa Brochu that it was impossible—couldn't be done. Lisa took on that challenge, and together with a team of academics and practicioners, developed the professional-level certification program which was approved by the board of directors in 1997 and implemented in 1998.

The professional certifications include Certified Heritage Interpreter (CHI), Certified Interpretive Trainer (CIT), Certified Interpretive Manager (CIM), and Certified Interpretive Planner (CIP). In order to apply for certification, the applicant must have a four-year college degree or the equivalent time in work experience. Each category is also designed for someone who has experience in that position, and requires applicants to pass several different types of requirements. All of the above categories require an open-book exam with multiple choice, short-answer, and true/false questions based on a minimum of six interpretive books in the certification library. The exam is designed like a scavenger hunt, searching through the texts to answer the questions. The intent is not to test the knowledge of the applicant, but to encourage them to become familiar with the books so they can use them as reference in the future and to provide a common starting ground with knowledge of available resources.

Other requirements include an essay exam, different for each category, and appropriate evidences of performance. For example: for the Certified Heritage

Interpreter category, applicants must submit a 30-minute video of an interpretive presentation and two examples of nonpersonal media the applicant has planned, designed, and/or fabricated. Once the application is complete, the essay exam and evidences of performance are sent to three experienced professionals for peer review. In order to get certified, applicants must achieve at least an 80 percent score on all the certification requirements.

The certification program was launched and began to attract applicants, and the NAI board of directors began to consider another category, Certified Interpretive Guide, which would be designed for entry-level interpreters. Early in 2000 I was the newly elected president of NAI, and I assisted Executive Director Tim Merriman in teaching a training session for naturalists employed by CruiseWest, which specializes in small cruises in Alaska and other destinations on the west coast. Tim had spent many hours attending interpretive training courses taught by Dave Dahlen and David Larsen, trainers for the National Park Service and U.S. Fish and Wildlife Service as well as Dr. Sam Ham of the University of Idaho. Tim was collecting the best interpretive methods and training already developed in order to put together certification courses for NAI. CruiseWest wanted to certify its naturalists as Certified Heritage Interpreters. However, we found that not all of them had the basic requirements for certification: a four-year degree or equivalent work experience. It became evident that NAI needed to design an entry-level certification (Certified Interpretive Guide) which would require applicants to take a course to get certified.

Tim hired Lisa Brochu, who had helped develop the original program, as a contractor for NAI, and by the end of 2000, they taught the first official Certified Interpretive Guide (CIG) course in Mexico. They then designed a CIT course to certify individuals to teach the CIG course. I attended the first CIT course in early 2001. They went on to create courses for all the professional-level certifications. Although applicants can complete the requirements on their own, attending a course allows the applicant to get some of the requirements out of the way, such as the video presentation for CIM, CHI, and CIT, as well as the open-book exam that participants are encouraged to work together on during the courses. It is also a chance for the interpreter to shore up their foundation of knowledge and skills to become better at what they do.

The CIG certification is designed for entry-level interpreters, docents, and volunteers and requires attendance at a 32-hour course taught by a qualified CIT. CIG applicants also have to pass the same open-book exam as the professional-level certifications, as well as give a 10-minute presentation the last day of the course and submit an outline of their presentation. The course begins with a history of the profession and NAI; then progresses to knowing

**NAI's first CIG course was in Mexico in 2000.**

your audience; knowing your resource; using tangibles, intangibles, and universals, the key elements of good interpretation; using themes, subthemes, goals, and objectives; and fitting in with the mission of your organization. The course ends with appropriate interpretive techniques and informal interpretation. Participants then demonstrate what they have learned by giving a thematic presentation on the last day, along with an outline listing goals and objectives as well as themes and subthemes.

When the certification program began, I personally was not eager to get certified. The video and test requirements seemed difficult to do on my own, and I did not see much personal benefit. The development of the CIG program and attending the CIT course changed all that. I had been working as a naturalist and doing some interpretive training for 20 years. When I was introduced to the CIG material, I discovered some large gaps in my interpretation foundation. Although I was good at my job, I wasn't conscious of why the interpretive techniques I did instinctively worked well with audiences, or why I wasn't more consistent in my programming abilities. I wasn't familiar with some of the social science research that formed the basis for good interpretation, and I rarely organized my programs using themes and subthemes. I used to do programs without much preparation, confident that I would do a good job. I'm sure most of the time I did fine, but now I have the skills to improve my programming. I also take the time to get organized beforehand so I can more easily connect with my audiences and keep their attention. I also learned techniques for teaching interpretive skills to any audience.

Since taking the CIT course I have had an opportunity to teach several CIG courses as well as a CHI course, which teaches the CIG material on a higher level along with interpretive writing and design of publications, exhibits, and wayside exhibits. I find the material challenging for people on different levels. For experienced interpreters, the course materials offer ways to improve skills and gain new perspectives. For new interpreters, the course is taught as a progression of skills culminating in their interpretive presentation on the last day. A Boston tour guide I met during another training I had taught took my CIG course in early 2004. It had been a year since I had seen her. In the middle of the course she was struggling with writing and using a theme and confessed to me that she had been working on this concept for a year, since I had first introduced her to it. Later that day, the light bulb went on and she finally understood how to use a theme in her program. When she came to do her 10-minute presentation on the last day, she was perfect; the first person I have given a 100 percent score. She spoke eloquently and succinctly about the significance of Lexington, Massachusetts' town green, how it was the beginning of our march towards freedom in 1775.

The last course that Tim and Lisa developed and launched in 2003 is the Certified Interpretive Host (CIH) program. With financial assistance from the Texas Parks and Wildlife Department, this course is designed to reach the support staff at any interpretive facility including maintenance workers, law enforcement personnel, ticket takers, and gift shop employees. This two-day course empowers these employees to become informal interpreters through the concept that every visitor encounter is an interpretive opportunity, and that they have a vital role to play in supporting the mission of their organization. At this writing, the CIH course is just beginning to be taught around the country. CITs can add teaching this course to their credential by taking an extra two-day training class. I predict it will have a huge impact in the quality of future visitor experiences at interpretive sites across the U.S. and overseas.

NAI's mission is to inspire leadership and excellence to advance heritage interpretation as a profession. The certification program is taking us by leaps and bounds towards fulfilling our mission. The program on all levels is certifying interpretive professionals and support staff in the design, management, and delivery of excellent interpretive services. It is an exciting time for the profession.

# 6

## TRENDS IN THE PROFESSION

### Current Trends

In 2004 Tim Merriman and Lisa Brochu identified 12 trends in the interpretive profession.[77] They include the following:

### 1. Organizations must do more with less.

This theme has been a recurring message during every period of recession, and will likely become the watchword in the near future as financial resources in the United States are committed to homeland defense and other government programs related to global security. This makes it imperative that interpretive professionals work smarter by being trained as interpretive planners who plan programming and media that more effectively achieves management goals and objectives.

Tom Marcinkowski introduced logic models to the environmental education community for analysis of environmental education programs.[78] The emergence of logic models in evaluation of programming came about primarily as a result of demand by the funding community. The W.K. Kellogg Foundation released a *Logic Model Development Guide* (2004)[79] as a way of "Using Logic Models to Bring Together Planning, Evaluation, and Action." Supporters of interpretive programs must be able to understand the relative benefits of those programs. NAI has adopted this approach in training of guides, managers, and planners with hopes of making evaluation a mainstream activity in alignment with Cable and Beck's 12th principle of being able to attract support. Secondarily, this approach provides positive reinforcement to interpreters and managers who can now receive immediate feedback and proof of value of their work.

### 2. Volunteers often comprise the front line and first contact.

NAI estimates that as many as 500,000 volunteers, docents, seasonals, and part-time workers comprise most of the front-line of heritage interpretation in the United States. Training these organizational representatives in how to help achieve the mission of their agency is critical if interpretive experiences must become more effective in achieving goals and objectives. NAI's Certified Interpretive Guide and Host courses were designed specifically for these markets.

### 3. Social marketing adds value to interpretation.

The curricula being used in current certification training for NAI and NPS embraces a social marketing model that involves moving people from curiosity to awareness to understanding and finally to stewardship. NAI's CIG training adds to that by focusing on teaching interpreters to write program scope objectives that can be easily measured as outputs, outcomes, and impacts using logic models.

### 4. Interpretation may have important economic impact.

Quality interpretive services may encourage guests to stay longer, encourage them to encourage their friends to visit, return more frequently, and spend more money, but more research is needed to document these anecdotal observations. Interpretive planning should take economic values into consideration and help organizations make better decisions before they invest in specific interpretive media.

### 5. Interpretation creates experiences.

Since Pine and Gilmore published their book, *The Experience Economy* (1999),[80] interpretive trainers have made the point that great interpretive programming usually uses the experience economy model. Brochu's book *Interpretive Planning: The 5-M Model for Successful Planning Projects* explicitly teaches a visitor experience model that begins with the decision to visit a site and ends with the commitment to behavioral changes.

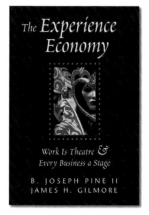

### 6. Interpretation builds advocacy for agencies and organizations.

Interpretation can target messages to both external and internal audiences that encourage support. Armed with the knowledge of the agency's mission, all employees of that agency or organization can make a difference in building constituencies that care about the resource and the agency itself.

### 7. Early childhood experiences create outdoor enthusiasts.

*Last Child in the Woods: Saving our Children from Nature-Deficit Disorder*[81] by Richard Louv in 2005 received acclaim from much of the interpretive community. The book points out the danger inherent in the extinction of experience among young people who rarely leave their homes to play outdoors. Interpretation has a key role to play in the exposure of more young people to heritage resources, for their own welfare and the good of society. Without that early engagement, the ability to connect with cultural and natural heritage in

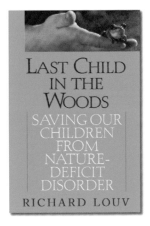

LAST CHILD IN THE WOODS
SAVING OUR CHILDREN FROM NATURE-DEFICIT DISORDER
RICHARD LOUV

later life may be lost. This trend also suggests that interpretation may become more valued by society in general if we do a better job of studying what we do and the impact it has.

### 8. Heritage tourism is expanding as a leisure activity.

According to futurist John Naisbitt,[82] global travel and tourism represents one-ninth of the world's economy. Interpretation has an obvious role and value in creating ecotourism experiences that help people understand their roles in preserving the places they enjoy recreationally. Recent studies in several southern states have shown birdwatching and ecotourism to have more economic impact than golf, the assumed leader in attracting tourists to the sunshine states. Heritage tourism around the world is destined to grow even stronger as 1.1 billion Chinese people begin to travel more and global access makes it easier for people to cross borders to learn about new places and peoples.

### 9. International interest in improving interpretation is on the rise.

Professional associations have started up in most developed nations in the past three decades as a network for interpretation. The First World Heritage Congress in Banff, Alberta, in 1985 was an attempt to create an international network that lasted until 1996. A new attempt at creating a global network that meets annually was established with the first Interpreting World Heritage conference in San Juan, Puerto Rico, May 1–5, 2006, sponsored by NAI doing business as the Association for Interpretation.

NAI's Certified Interpretive Guide course was first taught in La Paz, Mexico, in 2000. It has since been taught in Panama, Dominican Republic, Kenya, Mexico City and Cancun. This program is spreading in English and Spanish. Variations of the course have been taught in China as well. In time NAI expects it will strengthen the international network through common vocabulary and process as well as through trainers who work across borders.

The first Interpreting World Heritage conference in 2006 in Puerto Rico featured a distinctly international flavor. Participants from more than 30 countries included (pictured above, from left to right) Nikauly Vargas of the Dominican Republic, Bitapi Sinha of India, Maria Elena Muriel of Mexico, Meena Nareshwar of India, and Lidija Jularich of Slovenia.

### 10. Interpretation adds value to education.

Freeman Tilden wrote of education as "life-long learning."[83] In the modern context the word connotes state standards for education, required concepts in lesson units, and vocabulary lists for subject matter. The intellectual component of learning is important but the motivation to learn is emotional. Interpretation provides an experiential or emotional context for intellectual material.

### 11. Accreditation and standards add credibility to the profession.

Certification and accreditation programs are proliferating in all areas of the interpretive profession. By 2006, NAI had certified almost 4,000 individuals in six categories. NPS certifies constituents on specific competencies in 10 categories. These are used in some circumstances as criteria for promotion. The environmental education community has developed a certification program in some states and the North American Association for Environmental Education is working toward a certification program at the national level.

Zoos, aquariums, and museums have accreditation through the Association of

Zoos and Aquariums (AZA) and the American Association of Museums (AAM). There is interest in creating an accreditation program for nature centers and public lands as well. Measurable standards facilitate the assessment of program quality, which leads to the establishment of value. In these difficult economic times, the trend toward using measurable standards as an economic indicator of cost/benefit is likely to grow.

## 12. Interpretive audiences are changing.
American demographic trends indicate that Hispanic people will become a much larger group in the U.S. in a few decades.[84] Traditionally, their use of parklands has been minimal with emphasis on use as a family gathering place. Ethnic minorities will become the majority and may not value heritage preservation in the same ways than the more traditional Caucasian audiences of the past. This concern is driving many interpretive organizations toward strategies to involve diverse audiences at younger and younger ages.

Baby boomers are becoming senior citizens with broad travel interests and considerable disposable income. As a result, demand is likely to increase for interpretive programming, but the types of programming and media in demand may need to reflect the physical constraints of older audiences.

Interpreters have an opportunity and perhaps an obligation to develop strategies for engaging diverse audiences. Advocacy for natural and cultural resource sites in the future will depend on knowledge and interest in them by the entire electorate. Partnerships with other organizations will be needed in a continued effort to understand these new audiences and design experiences that meet their needs.

Virtually all of these trends in interpretation are part of larger trends of change in society at large. Staying connected with professional development opportunities available through the various professional associations is one of the most effective ways for interpreters to stay abreast of a changing world.

## The Future of the Profession
In his essay, "A Day with a Nature Guide" (1920), Enos Mills wrote:

> The aim is to illuminate and reveal the alluring world outdoors by introducing determining influences and the respondent tendencies. A nature guide is an interpreter of geology, botany, zoology, and natural history.

He gave a name to this natural tendency of humans that has stuck with the profession since Tilden wrote *Interpreting Our Heritage* in 1957. Mills and Tilden's books gave the profession a start on thinking about what we might become as a group, a tribe of professionals.

The future of interpretation depends more than ever on the professionalism of those who employ this approach to communication. Despite the challenges of economic recessions that result in cutbacks among interpretive staffs, in 2005 there were about 20,000 paid professional interpreters working in the United States. Twenty years ago the estimate was 5,000 individuals. Nature centers have proliferated in that same time frame from 500 to about 2,000. In 2005, the National Park Service employed 3,000 interpreters at 390 sites. Ecotourism companies are developing throughout the world and interpretive guides are essential to their business.

Books have proliferated in the profession and NAI's certification program encourages interpreters to keep abreast of the diverse sources available. NAI published *Management of Interpretive Sites: Developing Sustainable Operations Through Effective Leadership*[85] by Merriman and Brochu in 2005 with hopes that interpretive management will become a more important part of university curricula and in-service interpretive training.

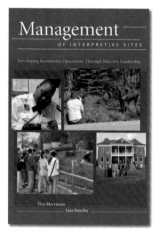

Partnerships have been of growing interest in agencies for several decades. Dr. Will LaPage, retired University of Maine professor, was one of the early advocates for partnerships (1994).[86] He demonstrated how partnerships work to an agency's advantage when he served as director of New Hampshire State Parks by seeking private/public partnerships that helped make that system self-sustaining.

Federal and state organizations are showing a great desire to work with private partners in creative ways. The National Park Service, Bureau of Land Management, Army Corps of Engineers, USDA Forest Service, and U.S. Fish and Wildlife Service each held partnership planning meetings between 2001 and 2005 to get input from potential private partners. Congress is pressing for increased collaboration and private/public collaborations are increasing.

In 2002 NAI began discussions with the U.S. Environmental Protection Agency (EPA) about bringing non-formal education and interpretive associations together with agency interpretive chiefs to talk about definitions commonly used in the field. EPA funded the Definitions Project in 2005 in cooperation with the U.S. Fish and Wildlife Agency through a grant to the Institute of Learning Innovation and NAI. This historic project brought together representatives from 18 professional organizations and six federal agencies to discuss similarities and differences amongst themselves in regards to how they approach interpretation and education efforts. Results of these historic meetings will be published by 2007.

## Challenges

Some great challenges face the interpretive profession in the near future. As agencies downsize and outsource interpretive services, the private sector and nonprofit partner organizations must fill the void. The need for interpreters and sound interpretive planning has never been greater. In 2005, about 150 colleges and universities taught at least one course in interpretation in the United States. Only about 20 universities had a major or concentration with two or more courses. The proliferation of jobs in the private sector without growth in academic programs has left many employers short of well-qualified employees. Academic units are reporting that even government sites that once had years of backlogs of applicants for seasonal interpreters, like Yellowstone National Park and Yosemite National Park, often have unfilled openings just before their busy seasons.

Baby boomers, the demographic lump in American society of people born between 1946 and 1964, are about to retire from federal service. Aliya Sternstein[87] reports that:

> Congressional auditors say some federal agencies are not doing enough to prepare for a wave of retirements. Some workforce experts say that the succession problem cannot be solved without spending more on training and hiring people from outside the federal government.

This wave of retirement is going to create great opportunities for advancement in the interpretive profession but there is some concern that there will be a deficit of well-qualified interpretive managers, planners, and researchers to take these openings. The expected trend is both a challenge and an opportunity for the profession to improve through better training and planning.

Research in the psychology, communication, and interpretive fields has gone on for a quarter of a century and serves as part of the foundation for the interpretive profession. George Millers' (1954)[88] Magical Number 7 Plus or Minus 2, Maslow's Hierarchy of Needs (1954)[89] and research on motivation, Thorndyke's studies of theme placement and value (1978),[90] and Cowan's (2000) Magical Number 4[91] provide a basis for decision-making in program planning. More research is needed to determine qualitative results of the effectiveness of various interpretive methods.

As a profession, interpretation has come a long way since Mills published *Adventures of a Nature Guide* (1920), but it still has much to do. Thoughtful research, excellent training, respected certification standards, quality workshops, and support of professional development are making a difference in these early years of the 21st century.

Despite the challenges that face the profession, the future has never been brighter for heritage interpretation. A professional, young or old, need only reflect on her or his personal responsibility for making the world a better place, for the profession will only be as strong as the individual interpreter. May all interpreters find the energy and heart to be the best they can be, for it is only with that personal commitment that a difference can be made by connecting visitors to heritage resources.

Enos Mills was a true visionary about this profession. In 1920 he wrote:

> Ere long nature guiding will be an occupation of honor and distinction. May the tribe increase!

Through the good efforts of interpreters everywhere, his vision of success lives on.

GUEST ESSAY

# Conducting Defensible Interpretation: The Role of Research
*by Carolyn Widner Ward, Ph.D.*

What is the role of research in interpretation? Research is the *key* to the survival and development of the discipline itself. Without tangible, defensible results from interpretive programs and services, interpretation itself will go the way of the dinosaur. In this day and age of limited budgets, personnel, and time, only those services with discernible results will continue to be supported. Research provides the glue that links our services, the interpreters, the audiences, and the managers together within the science of the practice of interpretation.

Interpretation is often considered to be a fringe visitor service without real, tangible benefits. As a result, the field itself is being increasingly marginalized in budgets and staffing. Despite ideas of what interpretation can or should do, a lack of "evidence" and demonstrable outcomes results in interpretation being the first to go when funding is low and the last to be considered when park planning is conducted. Historic functions and benefits of interpretation like education and visitor management are no longer demonstrably provided by interpreters, but instead are carried out by environmental educators and law enforcement officers respectively. Both of these groups provide tangible measurable outcomes of their services and thus are being increasingly supported over interpretation.

Resources are experiencing pressure from growing numbers of visitors while managers, faced with decreasing budgets, are asked to control behavior, protect visitor experiences, and provide for recreation opportunities for everyone. Amidst this climate, the key to ensuring the survival of interpretation is through providing services that clearly meet or address visitor, resource, and management needs. Making the discipline of interpretation unexpendable is the role of research.

The key to defending and ensuring the survival of the field is to critically examine what interpretation does, how it is done, and what results from it. In other words, conducting *defensible* interpretation is the key to the survival of our discipline. Research serves this purpose. Research is the element in the interpretive process that links all other steps and participants. It is both the first and the last. It begins the planning process by allowing interpreters to identify target audiences, understand and know the resource, and establish program goals and objectives. Research is also at the heart of the creative process. The design of appropriate messages that meet audience, resource, and management needs requires research. Research is also the final step in the process. It provides the measurement and assessment of whether or not goals and objectives were met.

For example, research sets the direction and helps establish what interpretation should do. From managers to field interpreters, it is through research that appropriate goals and objectives can be outlined for interpretive services. The *purpose* behind the program should always be able to be articulated within the framework of management goals and objectives. Interpretation conducted without a purpose is simply entertainment, and although we hope that our interpretive services are pleasurable and enjoyable, they are *not* simply a means to entertain visitors. "An interpretive program should exist for a reason, and the best reason is to fulfill one or more management objectives or goals."[92] Numerous researchers, authors, and practitioners echo this position. The National Association for Interpretation agrees with this and has added "purposeful" to the basic qualities of good interpretation. According to NAI, "If you can't state the goals and objectives for your program, there's probably no reason to be doing it."[93]

Once research has established what should be done, the second primary role of research is to guide how best to accomplish those objectives. What messages are the most appropriate identified target audiences? Which mediums are the most useful? In other words, research should guide the design and delivery of appropriate messages to meet audience, resource, and management needs. For example, does thematic program work more effectively to increase message retention than does a program without a theme? Will non-personal or personal interpretive services work better? Research is the key to answering these questions and guiding our interpretive efforts and services to best meet the needs of management, provide the services and information that visitors seek, and address the issues dictated by the resource. How we conduct interpretation should not be based on what we think works but what we know, based on empirical evidence, works. This role of research is especially valuable to field interpreters.

This idea leads us to the third primary role of research, to know whether or not the interpretive services accomplished what they set out to do. There seems to be a variety of perspectives on how research and evaluation in interpretation should be conducted, ranging from rigorous scientific surveys to casual observations of visitors' behavior. There have been many debates regarding the appropriateness of rigorous scientific assessment versus the more traditional, gut-level impressions about programs. This is similar to the discussion of whether or not interpretation is an art or a science.

Seeing the sparkle in the eyes of visitors and sensing the enthusiasm in the audience are both "traditional" methods of evaluation. Interpreters that have worked in the field for any length of time can tell you when their program went well. These "traditional" proponents often view scientific evaluation as minimizing the true impact and effect of interpretation to the heart and mind of the individual. After all, we are exposing the "soul of a thing"[94] to the heart of a person. How can this be measured, and doesn't the mere attempt to assess it degrade the spirituality of it? How can you measure and quantify art?

After having worked as an interpreter myself, I can certainly appreciate the spiritual nature of the art of interpretation. However, given the current climate of accountability and limited resources, interpretation must justify the time, money, and personnel it requires. Interpretation may be spiritual in nature, but it must also be accountable to the people it serves, the agency it represents, and the resources it interprets. Just as ministers or priests may be "called" to the church, they are still trying to accomplish particular goals and are periodically evaluated on their effectiveness in meeting those goals. It does not lessen their spirituality to be evaluated, but instead is an indicator of their commitment and dedication to their profession. Regardless of the specific methods used, measurement of the success of meeting the mission, goals, and objectives of the agency and the program is critical to maintaining support for interpretive services, increasing overall effectiveness, meeting audience needs, and protecting the resource and the visitor.

Research is the element in the interpretive process that links all other steps. It is the first, the middle, and the last. It begins the planning process by allowing the interpreter to identify target audiences, understand and know the resource, and establish program goals and objectives. It provides the guidance and direction for the design of appropriate messages to meet audience, resource, and management needs. Research is also the final step in the process. It provides the measurement and assessment of whether or not goals and objectives were met and by doing so helps establish future issues and goals thus closing the loop. Research serves to link the manager and administrator to the field interpreter, the field interpreter to the visitor, the visitor to the resource, and the resources to the overall program goals and objectives.

The role of research is to educate, to enlighten, and to guide. Research is conducted because we want to know more, and because we want to do better. It must be made applicable to the practitioner, the manager, and the public. It needs to answer useful questions, and ask the unanswerable ones. In order to understand the best use of precious economic, human, and biological resources, research must be adequately funded. It should not be treated as an external afterthought to programming, but instead included as an integral part of the process. The survival of interpretation depends on the critical examination of what is done, how it is done, and what results from it. Research is the foundation of the practice of the science of interpretation.

GUEST ESSAY

# The Role of Interpretation in International Tourism
*by Ted Cable*

*"In Nature's ennobling and boundless scenes the hateful boundary lines and the forts and flags and prejudices of nations are forgotten. Nature is universal. She hoists no flag of hatred.... Sometime it may be that the immortal pine will be the flag of a united and peaceful world.... He who feels the spell of the wild, the rhythmic melody of falling water, the echoes among the crags, the bird songs, the winds in the pines, and the endless beat of the waves upon the shore, is in tune with the universe. And he will know what human brotherhood means."*

—Enos Mills

Tourism is the largest and the fastest-growing industry in the world. Virtually every country in the world, and every state and province in North America, is making a strategic effort to attract tourists. Their motives are mostly economic because tourism has the potential to generate new revenue and jobs. Futurist John Naisbitt predicted that "the 21st century economy will be driven by three super service sectors: telecommunications, information technology, and travel and tourism."

As tourism flourishes, opportunities for interpretation abound. Interpretation programs, products, and services now exist in most tourism destinations. Interpretation in the international tourism sector traditionally has been associated with destinations such as national parks, large museums, historic villages, and battlefields. Now many mass-tourism destinations, ranging from beachfront hotels to alpine ski resorts offer interpretive services. Tourists in every major city in the world can find multilingual interpretive bus tours operated by such firms as Gray Line Tours. In some cities such as London, city tour guides must be certified to ensure that their knowledge of the history, architecture, and local culture is adequate and that they have the skills to communicate this information in an entertaining manner. Theme parks and cruise ships provide other popular and growing venues for interpretation programs that serve the mass-tourism market.

The fundamental principles of interpretation apply regardless of whether the interpreter is working with tourists or residents in Timbuktu or Topeka.

On the international scene, a heritage interpreter often needs also to be a foreign language interpreter. But, whether locally or internationally, interpreters always are interpreting meanings in things that are foreign— whether the language of the French or the language of the forest. Likewise, the benefits that individuals receive from interpretation are similar regardless of the location. Interpreters meet the personal needs of people in countless ways while touching their emotions and intellect. Interpreters give the gifts of joy, knowledge, beauty, and inspiration to all audiences, whether tourists or local guests. In the tourism sector, interpretation functions in a particularly wonderful way to enhance what might be a once-in-a-lifetime experience for a tourist. In many cases, such interpreters have the opportunity to enrich the lives of tourists by the busload!

Beyond the direct benefits to individuals in interpretive audiences, the role that interpretation plays in manufacturing high-quality tourism experiences is profoundly important on a global scale. This essay describes the significance of interpretation as it promotes biological conservation and world peace in the context of international tourism.

## Promoting Conservation

*Interpretation: Enhancing the Benefits of Ecotourism*
Conservationists and policymakers in many countries are attempting to attract tourism and use it as a tool to save natural areas. This approach is not new. Tourism played an important role in the justification and establishment of the early U.S. national parks and it is still be used as a conservation tool today. This natural resource-based tourism is often referred to as ecotourism. The International Ecotourism Society succinctly defines ecotourism as "responsible travel to natural areas that conserves the environment and improves the well-being of local people." Ecotourism is the fastest-growing sector within the tourism industry. In recent decades this rate of growth of tourism has been greater in developing countries. Richly diverse, but highly threatened biological resources often characterize these countries. Conservation faces many complex economic and political challenges in developing countries. Ecotourism is seen as one approach to saving these resources while contributing to the welfare of the local people.

The fundamental basis for ecotourism as a conservation tool is to provide an economic incentive for people to protect their natural resources. Harvested resources, whether timber, grass, monkeys, or elephants, all have important values to local people, many of whom may be subsisting directly on the harvest of these resources. People cannot be expected to forego this harvest without alternative resources or income being provided to them. The task is to make the elephant worth more alive than dead, and the living forest worth more than the logs it contains. Then alternative sources of food or income must be provided to the people.

Ecotourism can save resources and bring prosperity to people. When it works well, ecotourism can benefit the local people and the host nation by bringing in foreign revenue through the payment of fees and the purchase of local goods and services (e.g., permits, fuel, food, guide services, lodging). Tourism is a labor-intensive industry and the provision of the goods and services results in the creation of jobs. Besides generation of jobs and revenue from expenditures, ecotourism can result in significant donations from altruistic tourists who are exposed to the conservation needs in areas they visit. Firms that profit from helping people experience these natural resources also contribute to the cause of conservation. An example of excellence in this regard is the Galapagos Conservation Fund (GCF) established by Lindblad Expeditions, a travel company based in New York City. According to Dr. Sam Ham, communications campaign designer and trainer for the GCF project, $3.6 million has been raised to support conservation on the

**Interpretation helps alleviate pressure on the environment caused by ecotourism in the Galapagos Islands.**

Galapagos Islands. Lindblad also works closely with and makes contributions to such groups as World Wildlife Fund and RARE Center for Tropical Conservation, an organization involved in developing ecotourism opportunities around protected areas in Latin America. Some "green" travel businesses build contributions directly into the cost of their excursions. Other firms solicit additional financial or in-kind donations from their clients for nature conservation. For example, Wilderness Birding Adventures encourages clients participating on bird watching trips in Alaska to make a $1 per day contribution to the Alaska Bird Observatory, the Northern Alaska Environmental Center, or the Alaska Conservation Foundation. This donation is conveniently figured into the client's bill. This firm also makes a 10 percent donation to the American Birding Association on selected bird-watching tours.

Besides direct financial contributions, ecotourism sometimes benefits local people by contributing to the development of community infrastructures. Ecotourism organizations helped provide new bridges, clinics, water wells, electricity, schools, and other assets to help local communities, particularly as they prepare for an influx of travelers for the first time.

How can interpretation enhance the conservation benefits of ecotourism? Interpretation as part of ecotourism experiences contributes to conservation on several levels. By making the tourism experience more enjoyable, educational, and enriching, interpreters increase the value of the experience. Just as with other market commodities people may be willing to pay more or consume more when the product is perceived to be of high value. In this way, interpretation can encourage demand and keep the resultant revenue flowing into the host country and local communities. Moreover, a fundamental principle of interpretation is that it should provoke thought or action. Inspiring, convicting, and convincing interpretation can provoke political support and donations of time and money for the cause of conservation in these locations. Once-in-a-lifetime, possibly life-changing world-class experiences turn the heart of the tourist toward helping. An interpreter assigning meaning and significance to both the natural resource and potential donations may prompt gifts of appreciation and preservation. Also, as local guides and interpreters are hired, interpretation creates jobs and income for local families. These jobs, along with the modeling of environmentally responsible behavior and the interpretive messages being communicated, can build support for conservation among local people. When people understand that they have something unique and valuable to offer the rest of the world, they often take pride in their natural and cultural heritage and want to protect those resources for future generations.

If people in modern industrial countries want to preserve nature in poor developing countries, we are going to have to pay for it ourselves. Ecotourism provides a revenue-producing product and one framework for delivering payments to fund conservation efforts. Interpretation can enhance the tourism product, promote stewardship among local people and tourists, increase understanding and concern about conservation needs, and provoke expenditures and philanthropy.

*Interpretation: Limiting Negative Impacts of Ecotourism*
Like any powerful tool, ecotourism only works in certain situations. It is not always the appropriate conservation approach. Ecotourism is dangerous and can destroy natural resources and local communities if it is used unwisely. Infrastructure developments and the increase in people can pollute or totally eliminate the very ecosystems tourism was meant to save. Crime, disease, loss of traditional family roles and values, and other social problems result from misguided ecotourism efforts. Leakage of the economic benefits out of the host community by not purchasing local supplies and services, or not hiring

local guides and other labor, drains away the promised financial benefits.

To address these issues, travel industry associations, nature conservation groups, and international organizations such as the United Nations have established codes of ethical standards and codes of professional conduct to guide ecotourism providers and tourists. Countries such as Costa Rica, Kenya, and Australia have developed their own standards to reduce the negative impacts and maximize the benefits of ecotourism. For example, general standards from The International Ecotourism Society state that ecotourism should:

- Minimize impact
- Build environmental and cultural awareness and respect
- Provide positive experiences for both visitors and hosts
- Provide direct financial benefits for conservation
- Provide financial benefits and empowerment for local people
- Raise sensitivity to host countries' political, environmental, and social climate

Interpreters are distinctly positioned to achieve those aspirations and purposes. Interpreters teach people to travel softly with fewer negative impacts on the resource. They create positive experiences and their messages can raise awareness, respect, and sensitivity for cultures and their environments. As previously mentioned, interpreters can generate cash flow from expenditures, wages, and philanthropy for the benefit of local people and conservation.

Jacques Cousteau said, "People will only protect what they love." Interpreters help tourists see the beauty and value in landscapes, organisms, artifacts, and history. Like romantic matchmakers, interpreters bring together resources and tourists, create the appropriate mood, and raise levels of understanding and sensitivity to draw people closer to the resources and ultimately to learn to love them. If tourists care about the natural and cultural resources in places they visit, they will care for them. In this way, interpreters help maximize the conservation benefits and minimize the negative impacts of this growing industry.

## Promoting Peace

*The world is becoming a global village in which people from different continents are made to feel like next-door neighbors. In facilitating more authentic social relationships between individuals, tourism can help overcome many real prejudices, and foster new bonds of fraternity. In this sense tourism has become a real force for world peace.*

—Pope John Paul II

*Interpretation: Making Peace*

Tourism has been called "The World's Peace Industry." In 1988, The First Global Conference: Tourism—A Vital Force for Peace was held in Vancouver, Canada, to explore "new initiatives to further the goal of global peace through tourism." The premise of the conference was that "tourism transcends governmental boundaries by bringing peoples of the world closer together through understanding of different cultures, environments and heritage."

As the Cold War of the late 20th century was nearing an end, President Reagan gave a speech in which he said of the United States and Soviet Union, "Imagine how much good we could accomplish, how the cause of peace would be served, if more individuals and families from our respective countries could come to know each other in a personal way. . .." A few days later Secretary Gorbachev and President Reagan issued a joint statement saying, "There should be greater understanding among our peoples and to this end we will encourage greater travel."

The value of travel in bringing people together has been recognized for many years. Mark Twain wrote, "Travel is fatal to prejudice, bigotry and narrow-mindedness all foes to real understanding." Travel reshapes the mind of the traveler. As author Judith Stone wrote, "Travel is not only broadening, I've realized but burdening too. I carry these lives and places with me. But I'm grateful for the ballast; it's keeping me from tipping into total complacency." She goes on to note that travel changes the way we vote, shop, donate, and, in short, live.

It is not merely the physical movement of travel that brings forth the broadening and burdening. Rather, it is the illumination of the meanings and beauty of places and peoples that eliminates prejudice, bigotry, and complacency. This illumination is the goal and responsibility of interpreters in the tourism sector. We care more about places and people we know. We skim over and barely notice news of an earthquake or train wreck in a far-off land unless we have a personal attachment to that place or those people. Interpreters introduce tourists to new cultures and help them know the people. Interpreters touching emotional chords in the hearts of tourists evoke empathy for the local people and appreciation of their culture.

*Interpretation: Keeping the Peace*

"Blessed are the peacemakers." *(Matthew 5:9)*

Of course tourism is not always a unifying and enriching experience for the local hosts. Some communities and cultures do not welcome tourists. Some resent "rich tourists" walking through their villages spreading diseases and disrupting traditional village life. Tourism operators must be sensitive to the needs and desires of the host community. In this regard, The World Tourism Organization's Code of Ethics includes the following:

- The understanding and promotion of the ethical values common to humanity, with an attitude of tolerance and respect for the diversity of religious, philosophical, and moral beliefs, are both the foundation and the consequence of responsible tourism; stakeholders in tourism development and tourists themselves should observe the social and cultural traditions and practices of all peoples, including those of minorities and indigenous peoples, and recognize their worth.

- Tourism activities should be conducted in harmony with the attributes and traditions of the host countries and in respect for their laws, practices, and customs.

- Tourism activity should be planned in such a way as to allow traditional cultural products, crafts, and folklore to survive and flourish, rather than causing them to degenerate and become standardized.

Interpreters contribute to each of these ethical standards by promoting understanding and appreciation of the beauty and value of diverse cultures. Interpreters cause tourists to care about the welfare of the individuals, communities, and cultures they encounter in their journeys. As with natural resources, if tourists care about the people and cultures, they will care for them. In this way interpreters maximize tourism's potential for peace.

## Summary

Interpreters give gifts of understanding and beauty to travelers around the globe. These gifts have profound effects on the lives of tourists, as well as on the communities and countries hosting the travelers. These interpretation-driven changes in people foster the spread of stewardship and fellowship. Because of its ability to change human attitudes and behavior, tourism has been touted as a conservation tool to save nature, and has been called the ultimate peace industry. By communicating the values of natural and cultural heritage, interpreters enhance these benefits of international tourism. Interpreters, while enriching lives of travelers, cause them to be compassionate—cause them to care. Caring travelers contribute to conservation and peace. It is the privilege and the responsibility of interpreters to be conservation-makers and peacemakers throughout the world.

# A

APPENDIX:
CONTRIBUTORS
TO THE FIELD

Many poets, philosophers, teachers, explorers, and leaders over time influenced the intellectual communities of their times to foster education leading to interpretive communication. No single piece seems to be the origin of interpretation but all of them contribute a piece of the foundation for what we do in modern interpretation.

Thales, 640–546 BC, Introduced astronomy and water cycle

Democritus, 584–500 BC, Sound related to mathematics

Socrates, 469–399 BC, Questioning to seek truth

Plato, 429–348 BC, Learning by doing, interrelationship of life and learning

Aristotle, 384–322 BC, Natural sciences begin, advocated need for experience, discipline, and leisure in education

Cicero, 106–43 BC, Great orator, noted for rhetoric theory

Horace, 65–8 BC, Roman poet–philosopher whose poetry influenced social behaviors

Quintilian, 40–118 AD, Spanish–born Roman orator, rhetorician who believed in teaching rhetoric and valued experiential learning

Roger Bacon, 1214–1294, Popularized useful knowledge

Petrarch, 1304–1372, Promoted science and arts, spirit of inquiry

Erasmus, 1467–1536, Encouraged a humanistic approach to learning

Galileo, 1564–1642, Demonstrated relationship between cause and effect

John Amos Komensky Commenius, 1592–1670, Promoted use of sensory experiences and perceptions to facilitate knowledge and understanding with children

Sir Izaak Walton, 1593–1683, Encouraged outdoor recreation in the
  *Compleat Angler*

John Locke, 1632–1704, Believed in gaining knowledge through experimentation
  and observation

Sir Hans Sloane, 1660–1753, British Museum was started in 1753 based on his
  extensive cultural and natural history collections being sold to the British
  government.

Jean Jacques Rousseau, 1712–1778, Author/philosopher who recognized that
  learning is facilitated by play and direct experience

John Bernard Basedow, 1723–1790, Promoted informal education and field trips
  into neighborhoods nearby

Gilbert White, 1720–1793, Wrote about English natural history and interpreted
  flora and fauna

Johann Heinrich Pestalozzi, 1746–1827, Viewed sense perception as the
  foundation of knowledge and he taught observation

Frederick Froebel, 1782–1752, Writer and teacher advocated for object teaching
  and outdoor educational activities

John Bartram, 1699–1777, Started a botanical garden and published a journal of
  explorations of southeast U.S.

Mark Catesby, 1731, Published Natural History of Carolina

Karl von Linné, 1707–1778, Wrote Genera Plantarum and Species Plantarum
  establishing binomial nomenclature

Thomas Say, 1787–1834, First American-born naturalist, founder of descriptive
  entomology

George de Cuvier, 1769–1832, Leading French naturalist of his time and early
  comparative anatomy scientist

John James Audubon, 1785–1851, Dominant wildlife artist of his days who
  painted from observation of dead birds

Thomas Nuttall, 1786–1859, Naturalist who published on many undescribed plants

Constantine Rafinesque, 1783–1840, Turkish–born naturalist who published
  natural history books and had an early evolution theory

William Maclure, 1763–1840, Scottish–born geologist made the first geologic map
  of the U.S., considered father of American geology.

Alexander Wilson, 1766–1813, Scottish–born naturalist, writer, poet, and artist
  who painted many of America's birds

David Douglas, 1798–1834, Scottish–born botanist traveled the American west
  collecting plants and keeping a journal

Charles Darwin, 1809–1882, Naturalist who went on mapping expedition to South America and wrote "Origin of the Species in 1859 espousing evolutionary theory

Wilbur S. Jackman, 1855–1907, Wrote Nature Study for Common Schools

Liberty Hyde Bailey, 1858–1954, Led nature study movement at Cornell University

Mr. & Mrs. Charles Goethe, 1875–1966, Sponsors of Lake Tahoe nature programs based on nature guiding observed in Switzerland

Grant Sharpe, 1926–2006, professor at University of Washington and author of *Interpreting the Environment* (1982)

Chris Nelson, Founder and first president of Western Intepreters Association

Harold Wallin, professional with Cleveland Metroparks (1961), first President of Association of Interpretive Naturalists.

Howard "Howdy" Weaver, co-founder of Association of Interpretive Naturalists (AIN), submitted AIN's IRS application for 501c3 non-profit status (1965)

Gabe Cherem and Elizabeth Winzeler, authors of *Bibliography of Interpretive Resources* (1978)

Steve Van Matre, founder of Institute for Earth Education and author of *Acclimitization, Acclimitizing, Sunship Earth* and *The Earth Speaks* (1983).

May Theilgaard Watts, former director of education at Morton Arboretum and author of *Reading the Landscape of America* (1957)

Bill Lewis, National Park Service trainer, University of Vermont professor and author of *Interpreting for Park Visitors* (1962)

Sam Ham, professor at University of Idaho and author of Environmental Interpretation (1992).

John Veverka, planning consultant and author of *Interpretive Master Planning* (1994)

Ted T. Cable, professor at Kansas State University and co-author of *Interpretation of Cultural and Natural Resources* (1995), *Interpretation for the 21st Century* (2002), *Birds of the Great Plains* (2005), and many other titles

Douglas M. Knudson, former professor at Purdue University and co-author of *Interpretation of Cultural and Natural Resources* (1995)

Larry Beck, professor at San Diego State University and co-author of *Interpretation of Cultural and Natural Resources* (1995)

Joseph Cornell, author of *Sharing Nature with Children* (1998) and other titles

Michael Gross, former professor at University of Wisconsin–Stevens Point, and co-author of *The Interpreter's Guidebook* (1992), *Signs, Trails, and Wayside Exhibits* (1991), *Interpretive Centers* (2002), and other titles.

Ron Zimmerman, director of  at University of Wisconsin–Stevens Point, and co-author of *The Interpreter's Guidebook* (1992), *Signs, Trails, and Wayside Exhibits* (1991), *Interpretive Centers* (2002), and other titles

Lisa Brochu, author of *Interpretive Planning* (2003), and co-author of *Personal Interpretation* (2002), *Management of Interpretive Sites* (2005), and *History of Heritage Interpretation in the United States* (2006)

Tim Merriman, co-author of *Personal Interpretation* (2002), *Management of Interpretive Sites* (2005), and *History of Heritage Interpretation in the United States*

Alan Leftridge, author of *Interpretive Writing* (2006)

Carolyn Widner Ward, Humboldt State University professor and co-author of *Conducting Meaningful Interpretation* (2006)

Alan E. Wilkinson, co-author of *Conducting Meaningful Interpretation* (2006)

Through its awards program, the National Association for Interpretation recognizes outstanding achievements and showcases the successes of NAI members and others working to advance the profession of interpretation. NAI members are exposed to outstanding and inspiring programs and professionals. Below is a list of recipients of NAI awards.

### NAI Fellow *(In the 1990s the NAI Board of Directors chose to honor all previous AIN/WIA Fellows as NAI Fellows.)*

2006: Donna Pozzi
2005: Paul H. Risk
2004: Bob Jennings
2003: Tom Mullin
2002: Bob Hinkle
2001: Cem Basman
2000: Ted Cable
1999: Gail Vander Stoep
1998: Mike Legg
1997: Jim Covel
1996: Jim Goss
1995: James Gale
1994: Lisa Brochu
1993: Gary Mullins
1992: Mike Link
1991: Paul Fransden
1990: Sam Ham
1989: Ron Russo
1988: William Lewis
1987: Tim Merriman
1985: Dave Patterson
1981: Gabriel Cherem, Elizabeth Horn, Frank Podriznik, John Hanna, Roland Nagel
1980: Walter Jones, Ben Mahaffey
1979: Robert Young

1978: Jerold Elliot
1977: Harold Gilluame
1976: Nelson Bernard, Carl Holcomb, Patricia Eising Carlson, Arthur Wilcox
1975: John Brainerd, Donald Robinson
1974: Grant Sharpe
1973: Paul Goff, Paul Knapp Jr.
1972: Bryon Ashbaugh Stanton Ernst Sr., Charles Mohr, Howard Weaver, Roland Eisenbeis, Robert Kelly, Wiliam Colpitts, Kenneth Hunts, Bertalan Szabo, Frank Bunce, William Hopkins
1969: C. Kenny Dale, Alan Helmsley, Harold Wallin
1968: Robert Mann, Sigurd Olson
1967: Reynold Carlson, Walter Tucker, Garrett Ripley

### Excellence in Interpretation
1997: Christine Revelas
1996: Maggie Hachmeister
1995: Richard Pawling
1994: Althea Roberson

### Master of Interpretation
1997: John Luzader
1996: Ted Cable
1995: Bob Jennings
1994: Jim Pease

## Master Interpretive Manager

2006: Karen Green, Jay Miller
2005: Debra McRae, Donna Scheeter
2004: Robert Wittersheim, Denise Gehring
2003: Marianne Mills, Mona Enquist-Johnston
2002: Ken Gober
2001: Patrick Barry
2000: John Schaust
1999: Nancy Herwig, Ginger Murphy
1998: Jim Smith, Sarah Reding

## Master Front-line Interpreter

2006: Joanie Cahill, Wil Reding
2005: Foster Brown, Linda M. Yemoto
2004: Don R. Simons
2003: Scott Mair, Mary Bonnell
2002: Jason Neumann
2001: David Stokes
2000: Brian Cahill
1999: Ralph Naess
1998: Katie Ellis

## Outstanding New Interpreter

2005: Kelli English
2004: Janet L. Stoffer
2003: Jody Heaston
2002: Ginger Cox
2001: Leslie Witkowski
2000: Andrea Haslage
1999: Pete Stobie
1998: Jodi Morris
1997: Maria Daly
1996: Jon Spiels
1994: Mike Greene
1993: Craig Kirkwood
1992: Jennifer Emery
1991: Tim Cook
1990: Ken Bowald

## Outstanding Senior Interpreter

2006: Robert Stebbins
2005: Ralph Ramey
2004: Howard E. Weaver
2003: Donald Altemus
2002: Bertlan Szabo
2000: Forest Buchanan
1999: William Whitehouse
1998: Robert Hakala

## Outstanding Interpretive Volunteer

2005: Lori Spencer
2004: Mary Keefer Bloom
2002: Angel Gochee

## Meritorious Service

2006: Cathy Meyer, Jerry Bauer
2005: Chris Brabander, NIW 2005 Planning
Team
2003: Ray Novotny, Carol Leasure, Susan
Williams, Debbie Tewell
2001: Pamela Rout, Heidi Kortright, NIW
2001 Planning Team, Spring Training
Hawaii Planning Team
2000: Mary Ann Best, Amy Galperin, Dr. John
Burde, Sue Benson, Sarah Blodgett, James
Heitzman, Deb McRae, Vicky Wachtler,
Gary Warshefski, Doug Weeks, Linda
Yemoto, NIW 1999 Planning Team,
Spring Training Duluth Planning Team,
NIW 2000 Planning Team
1999: Gary Stolz, John Morris, Diane Jung,
Kristi Kantola, Jean Kinnear, Dominic
Canale, Amy Galperin, Costa Dillon
1998: Chan Biggs, Lisa Brochu, Alan Capelle,
Carol Cole, Bob Valen
1997: Rick Magee, Marsha Knittig
1996: Vem Fish, Sandy Lyons, Roy Geiger, Gail
Vander Stoep, Debra Erickson
1995: Corky McReynolds, Broc Stenman, NAI
Region 4 NIW Planning Team
1994: Brett Wright, Tom Mullin, Sarah
Blodgett, John Baines, Julie Carrol, Wil
Reding, John Schaust
1993: Karin Hostetter, Alan Leftridge, Mike
Nicholson, Paul Ferreira
1992: Duncan Rollo, Debbie Tewell, Ray
Tabata, Gabe Cherum, Robert Schneider
1991: George Tabb, Mike Legg, Dave Kulhavy,
Evie Kirkwood, Ann Wright, Larry
Contri, Michael Watson, Bob Budlinger
1990: Bob Jennings, Tom Mullin, Lee
Westerburg, Jim Malkowski, Fred Wooley,
Siah St. Clair
1989: Jann Young, Karin Hostetter, William
Randall, Gail Vander Stoep, Doug Ruth,
Dick Namba
1988- Tom Christensen, Ann Wright, Rich
Koopman, Dave Vincent, Jim Tuck,
Donna Pozzi, Paul Nelson, Lisa Brochu,
Mark Parmalee

1987: Tom Christensen, Ann Wright, Rich Koopman, Cem Basman, Mike Legg

## Outstanding NAI Product
2000: Region 5 ("Interpretive Undercurrents" book)
1998: Region 4

## Excellence in Interpretive Support
2006: Friends of Wehr, White Mountain Interpretive Association
2005: Friends of Algonquin Park;Theresa Coble, Mike Legg, and Pat Stephens Williams
2004: Friends of Hearst Castle
2003: Friends of Santa Cruz
2000: Friends of Sabino Canyon, USFS, Tucson, AZ; Friends of Great Smoky Mountains & Great Smoky Mountains Natural History Association, Gallatin, TN; Bruce Stebbins and Onondaga County Parks, NY
1999: Clarksville Riverfront Development Foundation,Indiana; Los Compadres de San Antonio Missions, Texas
1998: Friends of Holliday Park, Indianapolis, Indiana; Arkansas Departrnent of Parks and Tourism
1997: Hamilton County Parks, Cincinnati, Ohio
1996: KDSM Fox 17/Dan Nannen, Des Moines, Iowa
1995: Oxley Nature Center Association, Oklahoma
1994: Red Rocks Canyon Interpretive Association, Las Vegas, Nevada

## Community Interpretive Service
2005: McKay Lodge Conservation Laboratory, Inc.
2004: Lake Champlain Basin Program Steering Committee, Connexus Energy
2003: Friends of Crawford Park Dist.
2000: Susan Grace Stoltz, Friends of Creamer's Field, AK; Donald Pendergrast, Alaska Interpretive Services, AK

1999: Jill DiMauro, MNCPPC Montgomery Co., Brookside Nature Center, Maryland; Buckman Elementary School, Portland, Oregon; South Bend Audubon Society, Indiana; Friends of Huntley Meadows Park, Virginia; Barbara Norton, Wagon Wheel Natural History Association, California
1998: Friends of Bendix Woods and Spicer Lake, St. Joseph County, Indiana; Mike Edmonds, Dean of Students, Colorado College, Colorado Springs, Colorado; Pacific Gas and Electric Co, San Luis Obispo, California; Archeological Support Team (PAST), Arkansas

## NAI Special Award
2000: Bruce McHenry, Bruce Stebbins & Onodaga County Parks, KC DenDooven
Prior to 2000: James Eddy, Mary Lou Ferbert, Sharon Frandsen, John Hanna, Wendy King, Ron Parker, Jim Peters, St. Joseph County Parks-Indiana, San Diego County Parks, Philip Tedesco, Edward Thomas

## President's Award
2006: Roger Conant
2005: Mickey Willis
2003: Faith Duncan
2001: Enda Mills Kiley
2000: K.C. DenDooven

## Lifetime Meritorious Service
2000: D. Bruce McHenry

# APPENDIX: NAI/AIN/WIA BOARD MEMBERS

**National Association for Interpretation Board Members (through 2006)**

Mike Adams, Region 3, 2005

Cem Basman, VP Administration, 1994–1995; President, 1996–1999

Vicki (Loveland) Basman, Treasurer, 2002–2006

Sue Bennett, Region 3, 2001–2004

Mary Ann Best, Region 6, 1996–1997

Chan Biggs, Region 7, 1988–1989; VP Administration, 1989–1991

Bradley Block, Region 5, 2003–2005; Region Leadership Council, 2006

Sarah Blodgett, Region 9, 1991–1995; VP Programs, 1996–1999, President, 2000–2003

Tom Blodgett, Treasurer, 1996–1997

Chris Brabander, At-Large, 1999

David Bucy, Region 10, 1992–1993

Robert Budliger, Region 1, 1990–1988

Joan Cahill, Region 8, 1998–2001

Dominic Canale, Region 10, 1998–2001

Alan Capelle, Region 5, 1988–1991

Tom Christensen, Treasurer, 1992–1995

Carol Cole, Region 7, 1997–1998

Larry Contri, Region 3, 1988–1991

Jim Covel, VP Programs, 2004–2006

Gene Cox, Region 3, 1995–1997

K.C. DenDooven, At Large Rep., 2006

Sue Dickler, Region 2, 2002–2003

Costa Dillon, Region 8, 1990–1991; VP Programs, 1992–1993

Cindy Donaldson, Region 2, 1992–1996

Faith Duncan, At-Large, 2000–2001; Region 10, 2002–2005

Paul Durham, Region 2, 2000–2001

Janice Elvidge, Section Rep., 2004–2005

Vern Fish, Region 5, 1993–1996; VP Administration, 2004–2006

Paul Frandson, President, 1988–1991

Robert Fudge, Region 2, 1996–1997

Kim Garret, Region 3, 1997–1998

Ken Gober, Region 4, 1998–1999

Jim Goss, At-Large, 1998

Pat Gubbins, Region 7, 1999–2001

Karen Gustin, Region 10, 1989–1991

Neil Hagadorn, Region 10, 1988–1989; VP Administration, 1992–1993

Flip Hagood, At Large Rep., 2006

Lester Hodgins, Region 9, 2003–2005

Karin Hostetter, Treasurer, 1988–1989; Secretary, 1989–1993, Region 7, 2005

Sue Hughart, Region 6, 1997

Susan Immer, Region 8, 2004–2005

Anthony Ingraham, Region 1, 1995–1996

Bob Jennings, Region 6, 1988–1989; Secretary, 1994–1995; VP Administration, 2004

Harold Johnson, Region 8, 1992–1996

Wallace Keck, Region 6, 2000–2001Mike Kennedy, Region 5, 1999–2002

Evie Kirkwood, Region 4, 1994–1997; VP Programs, 2000–2003; President, 2004–2006

Karen LaMere, Section Leadership Council, 2006

Rachel Larimore, Section Rep., 2004–2005

Larry Larson, Region 6, 1992–1996

Carol Leasure, Region 7, 2001–2004

Mike Legg, Region 6, 1998–1999

Betsy Leonard, At-Large, 1998

Amy Lethbridge, Region 8, 2002–2003

Schafer Lewis, Region 6, 2002

Richard Libengood, Region 8, 1988–1989
Clare Long, Region 1, 2005; Region Leadership
    Council, 2006
John Luzader, Section Leadership Council,
    2006
Sandra Lyon, Region 2, 1989–1991
Steve McCoy, Region 2, 2004–2005, Region
    Leadership Council, 2006
Brook McDonald    , Region 5, 1996–1998
Christina Miller, Region 8, 1996–1997
Tom Mullin, VP Programs, 1994–1995; VP
    Administration, 1996–1999; Section Rep.,
    2003–2005; Section Leadership Council,
    2006
Ginger Murphy, Region 4, 2004–2005; Region
    Leadership Council, 2006
Mike Nicholson, Region 9, 1988–1991
Kathryn Noonan, Region 1, 1991–1995
John Osaki, Region 10, 1994–1996
Ron Osterbauer, Region 5, 1991–1993
Rick Parmer, Region 9, 1999–2002
Jim Peters, Region 7, 1993–1996
Jim Pollock, Region 10, 1991
Bill Randall, Vice President, 1988–1989
Sarah Reding, Region 4, 2000–2003
Christine Revelas, Region 9, 1995–1998
Donna Richardson, Region 1, 2001–2004
Stuart Richens, Region 3, 1999–2001
Debra Riley, At-Large, 2002; Section Rep., 2003
Merle Rogers, Region 6, 1989–1991
Jane Rohling, Region 10, 1996–1997
Duncan Rollo, Region 7, 1989–1993
Ron Russo, VP Programs, 1989–1991
Tim Schaffer, At Large Rep., 2006
John Schaust, Region 4, 1989–1993; VP
    Administration, 2000–2003
Pat Silovsky, Region 6, 2003–2005
Patricia Stanek, Region 3, 1991–1993
Bruce Stebbins, Section Rep., 2003–2005;
    Section Leadership Council, 2006
Doug Steigerwalt, Region 2, 2003–2004
Nancy Stimson, At-Large, 2000–2002
Debbie Tewell, Secretary, 1996–1999
Lynn Youngblood, At-Large, 1999–2002
Bob Valen, Treasurer, 1998      –2002
Gail Vander Stoep, President, 1994–1995
Mike Whatley, Region 1, 1997–2000
Fred Wooley, Region 4, 1988–1989
Ann Wright, President, 1992–1993
Jann Young, Secretary, 1988–1989
Lynn Youngblood, Secretary, 2004–2006

Ray Zimmerman, Region 3, 1994–1995
Ross Zito, Region 2, 1988–1989; Treasurer,
    1989–1991

## Association of Interpretive Naturalists Board Members

Frank G. Ackerman, Ethics, 1982–1983
Susan V. Allen, Secretary-Treasurer,
    1977–1978; Public Affairs, 1980
John Baines, Publicity Committee, 1977, 1980
S. Glidden Baldwin, Nominating, 1974–1975
    Nelson Bernard, President, 1974
Cem M. Basman, Region 1, 1985–1986
Mary Ann Bass, Region 7, 1985–1986
Bill Beckner, Professional Services Chairman,
    1979–1980
Lynn Beeson, Region 6, 1984–1986
Nelson T. Bernard Jr., Member-At-Large,
    1975–1976; Affiliations Committee, 1977
Chanler Biggs, Region 3, 1985–1986
Norman A. Bishop, Member-At-Large,
    1975–1976
Pat Bolman, Region 9, 1984–1985
John W. (Doc) Brainard, History, 1982–1983
Robert E. Budlinger, Professional Services,
    1982–1983
Frank H. Bunce, Affiliations, 1974–1975
Rita Cantu, Newsletter Editor, 1977
Patricia Carlson, President, 1976
Gabriel J. Cherem, Research, 1975–1977
William Chiat, Region 5, 1984–1986
Tom Christensen, Region 7, 1984–1985
William L. Colpitts, VP, 1965; Ways and
    Means, 1974–1976, 1980
Robert M. Day, Member-At-Large, 1975–1976
Mary Jane Dockeray, Great Lakes Region,
    1975–1976
Ann Dudley, Ways and Means, 1982–1983
Patricia L. Eising, Historian, 1974–1975;
    President, 1975–1976
Jerold E. Elliot, Professional Services,
    1974–1975; Training and Certification,
    1975–1977; President, 1979–1980
Stanton G. Ernst Sr., Newsletter Editor,
    1974–1976; Editorial Committee/
    Journal Editor, 1977; Journal Editor,
    1980
Roscoe T. Files, Northwest Region, 1975–1976
Paul Frandsen, 1984–1985 Region 3
Mike Freed, Professional Training and
    Certification, 1980

Harold Guillaume, SecretaryTreasurer, 1965

John Hanna, Rocky Mountain Regional Director, 1976; Rocky Mountain-High Plains, 1977; Secretary-Treasurer, 1979–1980

Anne E. Harrison, Professional Services, 1975–1977; Region I (Southwest), 1980

Robert W. Hawes, Region VIII (Simon-Kenton), 1980

Geoffrey Hayward, Research, 1982–1983

Carl J. Holcomb, Southeast Regional Chairman, 1971; Program Chair (annual meeting), 1975; Awards Committee, 1977

Elizabeth Horn, Region III (Northwest), 1980

Dorothy Boyle Huyck, Publicity, 1974–1976

Anthony A. Janda, Program Chairman, 1975–1976; Southeast Regional Director, 1975–1976; Membership Chair, 1979–1980

Walter A. Jones, Northeast Region, 1975–1976; VP, 1977–1978; President, 1982

Robert H. Kelly, Ethics, 1974–1975

Wendy King, Central Office Secretary, 1978

Richard Koopmann, VP, 1984–1985

William J. Lewis, Region II (Northeast), 1980

Andria Lukens, Nominating, 1982–1983

Thomas M. Maguire, Mailing, 1982–1983

Ben D. Mahaffey, Research, 1974–1975

James M. Malkowski, Interim Treasurer, 1979; Region V (North-Central), 1980; President, 1984–1985

James L. Massey, Affiliations, 1980

John G. Mauritz, Audit, 1975–1976; Workshop Steering Committee Chair, 1979

Bruce McHenry, Region 2, 1984–1985; Vice President, 1985–1986

R. Alan Mebane, Rocky Mountain-High Plains Region, 1975–1976; VP, 1980

Robert Mercer, Region 4, 1984–1985

Tim Merriman, Region 1, 1984–1985; President, 1985–1987

Robert Moeller, Editorial, 1975–1976

Richard E. Moseley Jr., Membership, 1974–1975

Thomas D. Mullin, Region 4, 1985–1986

Gary W. Mullins, Region 8, 1985–1986

Roland "Ron" Nagel, Training and Certification, 1974–1975; Ethics, 1975–1976

Theodore W. Navratil, Historian, 1975–1976

Christian Nelson, VP, 1975–1976

W. Graham Netting, VP, 1971

Susan J. Noble, Secretary Board of Directors, 1974

Frank Podriznik, Southeast, 1977; Awards and Recognition, 1980

Cynthia Potter, Newsletter Editorial, 1980

Gerald Potter, Northeast, 1977

William E. Randall Jr., Program and Arrangements, 1980; Awards, 1982–1983; Region 2, 1985–1986

Doris Ready, Program & Arrangements Committee, 1977

James A. Richardson, Northwest, 1977

Larry R. Richardson, Membership, 1975–1976; Ways & Means, 1977

Ralph H. Rudeen, Region III (Northwest), 1979

Marc Sagan, Member at Large, 1971

Chris Schillizzi, Affiliations, 1982–1984

Grant W. Sharpe, Ethics Committee, 1977, 1980

Judy Silverburg, Public Relations, 1982–1983

Thomas H. Smith, Affiliations, 1975–1976; Nominating, 1980

Wendy Souza, Membership, 1982–1983

David W. Stokes, Workshops, 1982–1983

David E. Traweek, Research, 1980

Walter A. Tucker, Editorial, 1974–1975

Rick Tully, Region IV (Mason-Dixon), 1980

Frances Twitchwell, Great Lakes Regional Director, 1976–1977; Region IX (Michiana), 1979

Peggy Van Ness, Office Manager, 1978; Executive Manager, 1981–1982

Jeffrey S. Wallner, Editor, 1982–1983

Harold E. Wallin, President, 1971; Nominating, 1975–1976; History Committee/Chief Naturalist, 1977; History Committee, 1979–1980

Howard Weaver, President, 1965; Awards Chair, 1974–1975

Dennis Whiteside, Region VII (South-Central), 1980

James Williams, Region 8, 1984–1985

Marilyn J. Williamson, Region VI (Southeast), 1980

Ann Winstead, Audit, 1974–1975

Fred J. Wooley, Region 9, 1985–1986

Ann W Wright, Secretary-Treasurer,
    1985–1986
Robert L. Young, Secretary-Treasurer, 1971,
    1974–1976, 1984–1985; President,
    1977–1978
Dennis Zawol, Region IX (Michiana), 1980

## Western Interpreters Association Board Members

Ira Bletz, Bay Area Chapter, 1982–1983
Anna Boccone, Fire Mountains Chapter,
    1985–1986
Bob Breen, Secretary, 1973–1975
Carleen Bruins, Bay Area Chapter, 1984–1985
Wayne Bryant, VP, 1970–1971
William Chiat, Midwest Chapter, 1983
Melissa Clark, Centennial Chapter, 1986
Doreen Clement, Historian, 1982–1987
Jim Covel, VP, 1979; President, 1987
Wallace R. Cromwell, President, 1973–1975
Art Crowley, Sierra-San Joaquin Valley
    Chapter, 1984–1986
Maryann Danielson, Secretary, 1970;
    Treasurer, 1971
Paul Ferreira, Treasurer, 1975
Robert Flasher, VP, 1987
Mike Freed, Oregon Chapter, 1981; President,
    1981–1982
Robert Garrison, Sacramento Valley Chapter,
    1984–1985
Kit Gillem, Southern California Chapter,
    1985–1986
Elana Hallett, Historian, 1977–1978
Hal Hallett, VP, 1977–1978; President,
    1979–1980
Karen Hardeston, Secretary, 1987
Sylvia Haultain, Northcoast Chapter, 1983
Jean Hawthorne, Treasurer, 1975–1976;
    Southern California Chapter, 1978;
    Historian, 1981–1982; Border Chapter,
    1985
Norwood Hazard, Historian, 1975–1976
Debbie Hill, Arizona Chapter, 1981–1983
Ron Hodgson, Fire Mountains Chapter, 1984
Eileen Hook, Sacramento Valley Chapter,
    1978; Secretary, 1979–1980
Henry Hornsby, Sacramento Valley Chapter,
    1981
Carol Hunter, Historian, 1979–1980
Paul Johnson, Secretary, 1975–1976

Carol Bylsma Jones, Centennial Chapter, 1984
Alan Kaplan, VP, 1980–1982; Bay Area
    Chapter, 1981; President, 1983–1987
Rich Koopmann, Secretary, 1977–1978
Richard Kuehner, President, 1976;Oregon
    Chapter, 1984–1986
Leo Larson, Northcoast Chapter, 1984
Dave Lewton, Bay Area Chapter, 1978
Mike Lynch, Treasurer, 1979
Norman MacIntosh, 1973
Joe Maurier, Centennial Chapter, 1981–1983
Paul Maxwell Treasurer, 1973–1974; Secretary,
    1974
Jil Mishball, Northcoast Chapter, 1985
Kelly D. Morgantini-Harness, Central Coast,
    1984–1985; Centennial Chapter, 1985
Simone Mortan, Central Coast, 1983;
    Monterey Bay Chapter, 1985
Christian Nelson, President, 1969–1971
Don Neubacher, Treasurer, 1985; Secretary,
    1986–1987
Mike Nicholson, Bay Area Chapter, 1986
Jill Nishball, Northcoat Chapter, 1986
Pat Parker, Midwest Chapter, 1984–1986
Barbara Peet, Treasurer, 1977–1978
Deborah Pinkerton, Sacramento Valley
    Chapter, 1982–1983
Donna Pozzi, Treasurer, 1980–1981
Mike Raney, Northcoast Chapter, 1982
Paul Romero, VP, 1975–1976; President,
    1977–1978; Southern California Chapter,
    1981–1984
Phill Roullard, San Diego Chapter, 1984;
    Border Chapter, 1986
Tony Schetzsle, Northcoast Chapter, 1978
Dave Simpson, Oregon Chapter, 1982–1983
Sam Smoker, Treasurer, 1970; Secretary, 1971
Mark Spencer, National Capital Chapter, 1978
Jack Surmani, Sacramento Valley Chapter,
    1986
Teresa Takahashi, Northcoast Chapter, 1981
Darwin Thorpe, President, 1968
Gordon Topham, Utah Chapter, 1981–1986
James Tuck, Secretary, 1981–1982
Dave Vincent, VP, 1984–1986
Doug Weeks, Oklahoma Chapter, 1982, 1985
Wendy Welles, Secretary, 1982–1984
Nord Whited, VP, 1973–1975
Linda Yemoto, Treasurer, 1982–1987
Jann Young, Secretary, 1983–1985

# ENDNOTES

1   Sinclair, Kevin, and Iris Wong Po-Yee. 2002. *Culture Shock! China: A Guide to Customs & Etiquette.* Portland: Graphic Arts Center Publishing Co.

2   Dewar, Keith. 2000. "An Incomplete History of Interpretation from the Big Bang." *International Journal of Heritage Studies* (6)2: 175–180.

3   Merriman, Bryan. 1998. *The Midnight Court/Cuirt an Mhean Oiche.* Chicago: Independent Pub Group.

4   Wikipedia, the free Encyclopedia. *Thespis,* 16 October 2005, <http://en.wikipedia.org/wiki/Thespis>.

5   Majors, Erin. *Daily Quotes,* 04 August 2006, <http://lightson.net/quotes2002.htm>.

6   Muir, John. 1896. "The National Parks and Forest Reservations," *Sierra Club Bulletin* 1(7): 271–284.

7   Darwin, Charles. 1859. *The Origin of Species.* New York: Prometheus Books.

8   Darwin, Charles, and Nora Barlow. 1958. *The Autobiography of Charles Darwin.* New York: Harcourt Brace Jovanovich.

9   Miller, Keith. "The West: George Catlin and Native Americans in the West: An Apologist Way of Life" *History News Network*, 16 October 2005, <http://www.hnn.us/articles/635.html>.

10  Russell, Charles Marion. *Meet C.M. Russell,* 04 August 2006, <http://www.cmrussell.org>.

11  Remington, Frederic. 1979. *The Collected Writings Of Frederic Remington.* New York: Doubleday.

12  Wolfe, Linnie Marsh. 1946. *Son of the Wilderness: The Life of John Muir.* New York: Alfred A. Knopf.

13  Strong, Kenneth. 1995. *Ox Against the Storm: A Biography of Tanaka Shozo, Japan's Conservationist Pioneer.* Kent: Japan Library.

14   Drummond, Alexander. 1995. *Enos Mills: Citizen of Nature*. Niwot: University Press of Colorado.

15   Mills, Enos. 1909. *The Story of a Thousand Year Pine*. Estes Park: Temporal Mechanical Press.

16   Mills, Enos. 1920. *Adventures of a Nature Guide*. Estes Park: Temporal Mechanical Press.

17   Shankland, Robert. 1976. *Steve Mather of the National Parks*. 3d ed. New York: Alfred A. Knopf.

18   Mackintosh, Barry. *The National Park Service: A Brief History*, 07 August 2006, <http://www.cr.nps.gov/history/hisnps/NPSHistory/npshisto.htm>.

19   USDA Forest Service. *Smokey Bear and Fire Prevention*, 7 August 2006 <http://www.fs.fed.us/r9/wayne/facts/smokey_bear.html>.

20   Morris, Mark Stanley. 1974. *A Method for Evaluating Interpretive Activities*. Thesis. California State University at Chico.

21.  Barber, Dee Seton. *Ernest Thompson Seton: His Life and His Legacies*, 07 August 2006, <http://www.etsetoninstitute.org/SETONBIO.HTM>.

22   Sharpe, Grant, et al. 1982. *Interpreting the Environment*. New York: John Wiley & Sons.

23   Silber, K. 1965. *Pestalozzi: The Man and His Work*. 2nd ed. London: Routledge and Kegan Paul.

24   Pinloche, A. 1901. *Pestalozzi and the Foundation of the Modern School*. New York: Charles Scribners Sons.

25   Sharpe, Grant, et al. 1982. *Interpreting the Environment*. New York: John Wiley & Sons.

26   Weaver, Howard E. *State Park Naturalist Programs: Their History, Present Status, and Recommendations for the Future*. Unpublished doctoral dissertation. Ithaca, New York: Cornell University Library.

27   Sharpe, Grant, et al. 1982. *Interpreting the Environment*. New York: John Wiley & Sons.

28   Dabney, Walter D. 1984. "Travels with Freeman." *Interpretation: From Tilden to Today*. National Park Service.

29   Sharpe, Grant, et al. 1982. *Interpreting the Environment*. New York: John Wiley & Sons.

30   Lewis, William J. 1960. *Interpreting for Park Visitors*. Fort Washington, PA: Eastern National Park and Monument Association.

31   Knudson, Douglas M., Ted T. Cable, and Larry Beck. 1995. *Interpretation of Cultural and Natural Resources*. State College, PA: Venture Publishing.

32  Beck, Larry, and Ted Cable. 1998. *Interpretation for the 21st Century: Fifteen Guiding Principles for Interpreting Nature and Culture.* Champaign, IL: Sagamore Publishing.

33  Ham, Sam. 1992. *Environmental Interpretation: A Practical Guide for People with Big Ideas and Small Budgets.* Golden, CO: North American Press.

34  Dorrance, John. "The Makings and Musing of a Master Interpreter." *Legacy* 11(5): 10–12, 32–39.

35  Gross, Mike, Ron Zimmerman, et al. 2003. *Interpretive Centers: The History, Design, and Development of Nature and Visitor Centers.* Madison: University of Wisconsin Press.

36  Brochu, Lisa, and Tim Merriman. 2002. *Personal Interpretation: Connecting Your Audience to Heritage Resources.* Fort Collins, CO: InterpPress.

37  Brochu, Lisa. 2003. *Interpretive Planning: The 5-M Model for Successful Planning Projects.* Fort Collins, CO: InterpPress.

38  Evans, Brent, and Carolyn Chipman Evans. 2004. *The Nature Center Book: How to Create and Nurture a Nature Center in Your Community.* Fort Collins, CO: InterpPress.

39  Merriman, Tim, and Lisa Brochu. 2005. *Management of Interpretive Sites: Developing Sustainable Operations Through Effective Leadership.* Fort Collins, CO: InterpPress.

40  Leopold, Aldo. 1949. *A Sand County Almanac.* London: Oxford University Press, Inc.

41  Carson, Rachel. 1962. *The Silent Spring.* New York: Houghton Mifflin Co.

42  Schaller, George. 1972. *The Serengeti Lion: A Study of Predator-Prey Relations.* Chicago: University of Chicago Press.

43  Schaller, George. 1980. *Stones of Silence.* London: Andre Deutsch.

44  Schaller, George. 1964. *Year of the Gorilla.* Chicago: University of Chicago Press.

45  Schaller, George. 1993. *The Last Panda.* Chicago: The University of Chicago Press.

46  The Museum of Broadcast Communications. *Watch Mr. Wizard: U.S. Children's Science Program,* 30 October 2005, <http://www.museum.tv/archives/etv/W/htmlW/watchmrwiz/watchmrwiz.htm>.

47  Bill Nye The Science Guy. *Bill Nye The Science Guy,* 30 October 2005, <http://www.billnye.com>.

48  Spring Wings Bird Festival. *John Acorn, Acorn the Nature Nut,* 19 November 2005, <http://www.springwings.org/jacorn.pdf>.

49  Internet Movie Database. *Richard Attenborough's Ghandi,* 19 November 2005, <http://www.imdb.com/title/tt0083987>.

50    The British Broadcasting Corporation. 1954–1964. *Zoo Quest.*

51    Attenborough, Sir David. *Life on Earth,* 19 November 2005, <http://www.bbc.co.uk/nature/programmes/who/david_attenborough.shtml>.

52    Costner, Kevin, director. 1990. *Dances with Wolves.* Orion Pictures.

53    Columbia Broadcasting System. 1953–1957. *You are There.*

54    National Broadcasting Company. 1963–1988. *Mutual of Omaha's Wild Kingdom.*

55    Burns, Ken. *Ken Burns: Shop PBS,* 19 November 2005, <http://www.shoppbs.org/family/index.jsp?categoryId=1412587&clickid=lftnav_sbs_txt>.

56    JustDisney.com. *Disneyland's History,* 19 November 2005, <http://www.justdisney.com/disneyland/history.html>.

57    JustDisney.com. *Disneyland's History,* 19 November 2005, <http://www.justdisney.com/disneyland/history.html>.

58    JustDisney.com. *Disneyland's History,* 19 November 2005, <http://www.justdisney.com/disneyland/history.html>.

59    JustDisney.com. *Disneyland's History,* 19 November 2005, <http://www.justdisney.com/disneyland/history.html>.

60    Solomon, John. 1995. "Rangers Returned from Layoff, Jetted Down to Disney World." *Boulder Daily Camera,* December 9.

61    Sea World Adventure Parks. *Sea World Park History,* 19 November 2005, <http://www.seaworld.com/seaworld/ca/dp_park_history.aspx>.

62    National Geographic Online. *National Geographic: Birth of the Society,* 19 November 2005, <http://www.nationalgeographic.com/birth>.

63    Otlaw Women. *Florence Merriam Bailey*, 19 November 2005, <http://www.outlawwomen.com/FlorenceMerriamBailey.htm>.

64    Johnson, Cathy. *The Historic Naturalists,* 19 November 2005, <http://www.epsi.net/graphic/historic.html>.

65    Lynch, Michael. *History of the California State Park Rangers,* 19 November 2005, <http://www.angelfire.com/ks3/bvst21/ranger.htm>.

66    Albright, Horace, and Robert Cahn. 1985. *The Birth of the National Park Service.* Salt Lake City: Howe Brothers Publishing.

67    Albright, Horace, and Frank Taylor. 1928. *Oh Ranger! A Book About the National Parks.* Stanford: Stanford University Press.

68    Albright, Horace, and Frank Taylor. 1928. *Oh Ranger! A Book About the National Parks.* Stanford: Stanford University Press.

69    Association of Interpretive Naturalists. 1958. Archives.

70    Nelson, Chris. 2000. History of WIA audio tape. NAI Archives.

71   Mills, Enos. 1920. *Adventures of a Nature Guide*. Estes Park: Temporal Mechanical Press.

72   Association for Heritage Interpretation. *Home Page*, 19 November 2005, <http://www.heritage-interpretation.org.uk>.

73   Asociacion para la Interpretacion del Patrimonio. *Home Page*, 19 November 2005, <http://www.interpreciondelpatrimonio.com>.

74   Interpretive Association of Australia. *Home Page*, 19 November 2005, <http://www.interpretationaustralia.asn.au>.

75   Interpretation Canada. *Home Page*, 19 November 2005, <http://www.interpcan.ca/about.html>.

76   Interpret Europe. *Home Page*, 19 November 2005, <http://www.geographie.uni-freiburg.de/ipg/forschung/ap6/interpret-europe>.

77   Merriman, Tim, and Lisa Brochu. 2004. "Twelve Trends in the Interpretive Profession." *Journal of Interpretation Research* 9(2): 65–72.

78   Marcinkowski, Thomas. 2004. *Using a Logic Model to Review and Analyze an Environmental Education Program*. Monograph Series, Volume 1. North American Association of Environmental Education.

79   W.K. Kellogg Foundation. 2004. *Logic Model Development Guide*. Washington, D.C.: W.K. Kellogg Foundation.

80   Pine II, Joseph, and James H. Gilmore. 1999. *The Experience Economy: Work is Theatre & Every Business a Stage*. Boston: Harvard Business School Press.

81   Louv, Richard. 2005. *Last Child in the Woods: Saving Our Children from Nature Deficit Disorder*. Chapel Hill: Algonquin Books of Chapel Hill.

82   Naisbitt, John. 1995. *Global Paradox*. New York: Avon Books.

83   Tilden, Freeman. 1977. *Interpreting Our Heritage*, 3rd ed. Chapel Hill, NC: University of North Carolina Press.

84   Texas A&M University, Recreation Park & Tourism Sciences. *The Texas Hispanic Population*, 08 August 2006, <http://ruralsoc.tamu.edu/hrp.htm>.

85   Merriman, Tim, and Lisa Brochu. 2005. *Management of Interpretive Sites*. Fort Collins, CO: InterpPress.

86   LaPage, W. F. 1994. *Partnerships for Parks: To Form a More Perfect Union—A Handbook for Building and Guiding Park Partnerships*. Tallahassee, FL: National Association of State Park Directors.

87   Sternstein, Aliya. *5 Tips for Nurturing the Next Generation*, 05 September 2005, <http://www.fcw.com/article90650-09-05-05-Print>.

88   Miller, George A. "The Magical Number Seven, Plus or Minus Two: Some Limits on Our Capacity for Processing Information." *Psychological Review* 63(2): 81–9.

89  Maslow, Abraham. 1954. *Motivation and Personality*. New York: Harper.

90  Thorndyke, P. 1977. "Cognitive Structures in Comprehension and Memory of Narrative Discourse." *Cognitive Psychology* 9: 77–110.

91  Cowan, N. 2000. "The Magical Number 4 in Short-term Memory: A Reconsideration of Mental Storage Capacity." *Behavioral and Brain Sciences* 24(1): 87–114.

92  Huggins, R. 1986. "Going for the Gold." In G. Machlis (ed.), *Interpretive Views*. Washington, DC: National Parks and Conservation Association. 65-70.

93  Brochu, Lisa, and Tim Merriman. 2000. *Interpretive Guide Training Workbook*. Fort Collins, CO: National Association for Interpretation.

94  Tilden, Freeman. 1977. *Interpreting Our Heritage,* 3rd ed. Chapel Hill, NC: University of North Carolina Press.

# INDEX